Facts and Photos for Readers of All Ages

CONFEDERATE
SOLDIERS

in the American Civil War

Mark Hughes

Savas Beatie
California

© 2019, 2021 by Mark Hughes

Library of Congress Cataloging-in-Publication Data

Names: Hughes, Mark, 1951- author.
Title: Confederate Soldiers in the American Civil War: Facts and Photos for Readers of All Ages / by Mark Hughes.
Description: First edition. | El Dorado Hills, California : Savas Beatie LLC, 2017. | Includes bibliographical references and index.
Identifiers: LCCN 2017043003| ISBN 9781611213416 (pbk: alk. paper) | ISBN 9781611213423 (ebk)
Subjects: LCSH: Soldiers--Confederate States of America. | United States—History--Civil War, 1861-1865. | Confederate States of America. Army. | Confederate States of America. Army—Military Life.
Classification: LCC E607.H84 2017 | DDC 973.7/42—dc23

LC record available at https://lccn.loc.gov/2017043003

Second Edition, First Printing

SB

Savas Beatie
989 Governor Drive, Suite 102
El Dorado Hills, CA 95762
916-941-6896 / www.savasbeatie.com / sales@savasbeatie.com

Savas Beatie titles are available at special discounts for bulk purchases in the United States by corporations, institutions, and other organizations. For more details, please contact Savas Beatie at the above address, e-mail us at sales@savasbeatie.com, or visit our dynamic website at www.savasbeatie.com for additional information.

Proudly published, printed, and warehoused in the United States of America.

To my wife, Patricia (Patty) McDaniel Hughes, and our daughter,
Anna Grace Hughes, without whose support and encouragement
I could not have written this book.

And in memory of my parents:
Clara Humphries Hughes, who introduced me to the joys of reading,
and Sidney Jackson (Jack) Hughes, who taught me the value of hard work.

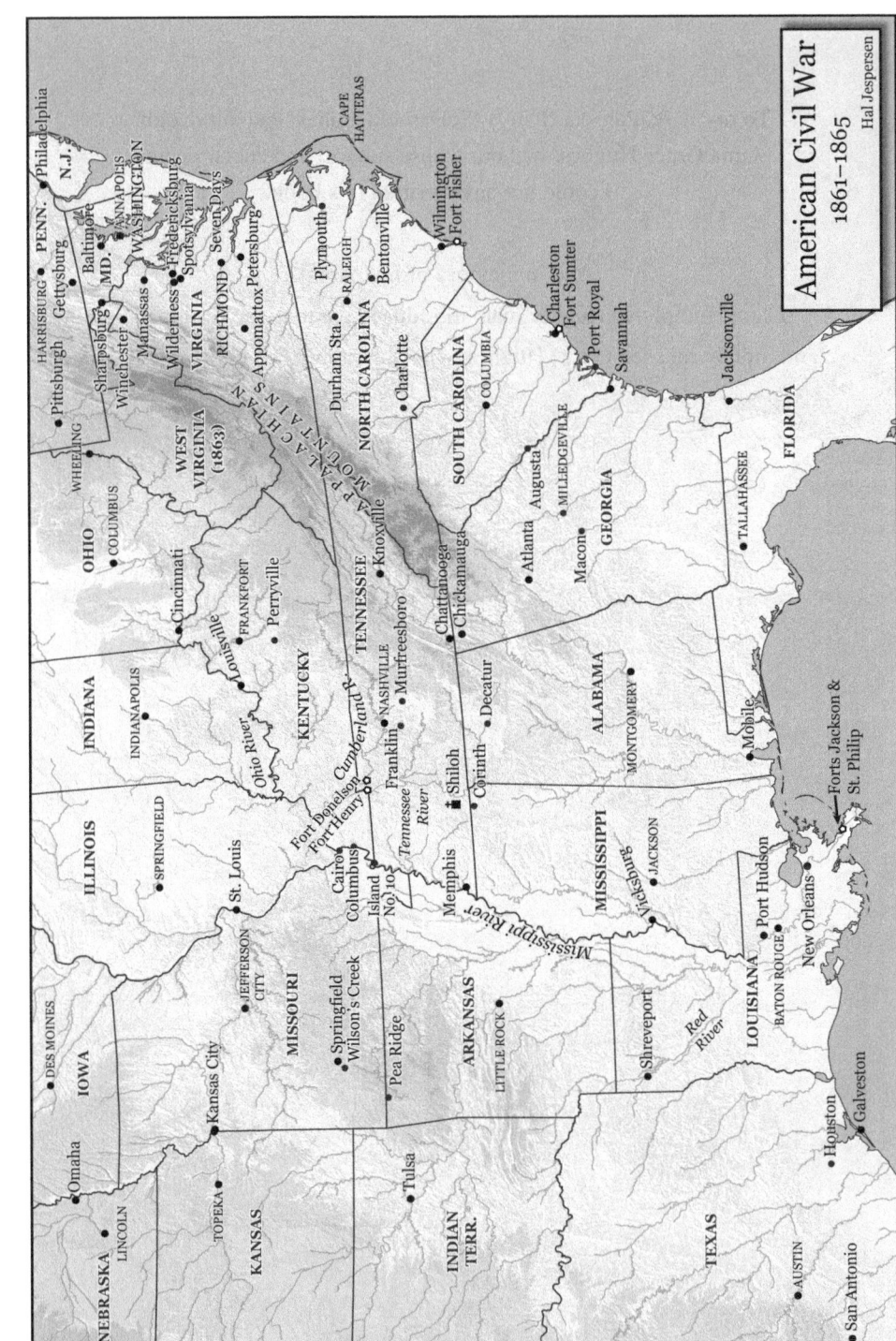

American Civil War
1861–1865

Hal Jespersen

Table of Contents

Introduction   vi

Acknowledgments   vi-vii

The Coming Storm   1

Enlisting for War   3

They Called Him Johnny Reb   6

A Soldier's Life   9

Organization of the Confederate Armies   16

A Concise Timeline of the American Civil War   20

Numbers and Losses   25

Photography   27

Weapons of War   32

Battles and Battlefields   38

Technology and the Civil War   55

Forts   61

Caring for the Sick and Wounded   66

Prisoners of War   71

The War on the Water   78

The Home Front   85

The War Ends   93

Remembering the War, Healing the Wounds   97

Gallery of Confederate Soldiers (arranged by state)   101

To the Last Man: The Final Confederate Soldier   136

Researching Your Confederate Ancestor   137

Glossary of Civil War Terms   140

Civil War Points of Interest   143

Index   156

About the Author   160

Introduction

After publication of *The New Civil War Handbook: Facts and Photos for Readers of All Ages* in 2009, a number of people asked me what I would write next. I had an abundance of excellent photographs and other material that could not be squeezed into the *Handbook*. I considered writing a book about Civil War soldiers, but unfortunately several serious eye surgeries delayed my writing plans.

Fortunately, by the time Theodore P. Savas, the managing director of Savas Beatie, contacted me about writing a book on Confederate soldiers, I had learned techniques that helped me compensate for my deteriorating vision. A number of books written by former Confederate soldiers had been digitalized and placed online. I was able to download these books and use my computer to enlarge the type and often change the type's font so I could read them.

Researching and writing this book helped me cope with the unexpected end of my 43-year career as an electronic technologist.

Acknowledgments

In my search for Civil War images, I received generous assistance from Deborah S. Wood, Museum Curator at Wilson's Creek National Battlefield; Troy Banzhaf, Supervisory Park Ranger at Pea Ridge National Military Park; John W. Guss, Site Manager at Bennett Place State Historic Site; Ms. Jodean Rousey Murdock, museum technician at the Rock Island Arsenal Museum; Mr. Eric N. Blevins, photographer at the North Carolina Museum of History; Colonel Diane B. Jacob, head of Archives & Records Management at the Virginia Military Institute.

Libby Stone, Public Services Librarian at Morris Library of Gaston College provided invaluable assistance, as did Sharon Stack and her staff at Mauney Memorial Library. Working with Ted Savas and his staff at Savas Beatie for the last ten years has been a pleasure. Marketing Director Sarah Keeney made many valuable suggestions about where and how to sell my books. She also served as my contact with Savas Beatie during the publication of this book. Renee Morehouse and Sarah Closson arrange book signings, programs, and interviews, and administrator Stephanie Ferro keeps things in order, and accounts manager Donna Endacott keeps my books on the shelves.

The material presented in *Confederate Soldiers of the American Civil War* was obtained from a variety of sources, the most prominent being: The U.S. War Department's *The War of the Rebellion: A Compilation of the Official Records*; the U.S. Surgeon General Office's *Medical and Surgical History of the War of the Rebellion*; Frederick Dyer's *Compendium of the War of the Rebellion*; and Mark Boatner's *Civil War Dictionary*. The primary source for the material about the Confederate soldiers in this book was the soldier's Compiled Service Record from the National Archives. Books written by former Confederate soldiers and material supplied by the soldiers' descendants supplemented the records from the National Archives.

Special thanks go to my mentor, Dr. L. David Norris, Professor Emeritus of History at Southeastern Oklahoma State University. Dr. Norris encouraged me to write my first book; this is my sixth. I would never have considered writing without his encouragement.

Finally, my wife, Patricia McDaniel Hughes, and my daughter, Anna Grace Hughes, were invaluable sources of support, gracefully accompanying me on research trips to various archives, libraries, cemeteries, and battlefields. They have driven me to book signings, programs, and interviews. I could have never completed this book without their help and understanding.

The Coming Storm

The Southern states that would form the Confederacy were mostly agrarian when the Civil War broke out. The North was caught up in a wave of industrialization, while most Southerners prospered as a direct result of agricultural. The population of the Southern Confederacy was slightly more than 9,000,000, but some 3,500,000 were slaves. The North, on the other hand, had a population of about 22,000,000.

There were many causes for the Civil War, with the issue of slavery, as manifested in the politics of the day, perhaps the most important of all. The two sections had uncompromising differences over the ability of the national government in Washington to stop slavery from spreading in the territories that had yet to become states.

The election of 1860, a four-way race that split apart the vote, was one of the most important in our nation's history. Abraham Lincoln's name was not even on the ballots in the Southern states. The election of Lincoln, who ran on a platform to keep slavery out of the territories, was viewed as a direct threat by many in the South. As a result, seven slave states in the Deep South seceded and formed the Confederate States of America, followed after the firing on Fort Sumter by four more:

South Carolina: December 20, 1860
Mississippi: January 9, 1861
Florida: January 10, 1861
Alabama: January 11, 1861
Georgia: January 19, 1861
Louisiana: January 26, 1861
Texas: February 1, 1861
Virginia: April 17, 1861
Arkansas: May 6, 1861

North Carolina: May 20, 1861
Tennessee: June 8, 1861

The new Lincoln administration refuses to recognize the legality of secession.

In April 1861, Maj. Robert Anderson commands Fort Sumter in the harbor of Charleston, South Carolina, a stronghold Lincoln has promised to re-supply. When Anderson refuses Confederate demands to surrender the fort, Confederate Gen. P. G. T. Beauregard orders artillery batteries to open fire. The fort surrenders soon thereafter.

The attack convinces President Lincoln to call up 75,000 volunteers to put down the rebellion, a call that spreads a wave of patriotism across both North and South.

Southern men by the tens of thousands flock to join and defend the new Confederacy to preserve its economic system, and especially their native states. None of them truly understand the sacrifices they will be asked to bear.

Enlisting for War

April 12, 1861. General P. G. T. Beauregard opens fire on the small garrison manning Fort Sumter in Charleston harbor. The fort hauls down the Stars and Stripes and surrenders the next day. The welcome news spreads like wild fire across the South, and prompts men by the thousands to flock to nearby towns to enlist in the war.

Most of the men join for what they see as the sheer excitement of going to war. To them, it is something of a lark—the great adventure of their lives. Many of their fathers and grandfathers served in the American Revolution or the War of 1812, and this was now their chance to become soldiers and "see the elephant," which means combat.

Enlisting at Natchez, 1861. These volunteers are enlisting at Natchez, Mississippi, in the spring of 1861. The have no idea what awaits them. *Miller, Photographic History of the Civil War*

The Hempstead Rifles, Company B, of the 3rd Arkansas Infantry. The unit originally organizes as a volunteer company in the 8th Regiment, Arkansas State Militia, on January 12, 1860. Here, its members are about to march out of Washington, Arkansas. The Hempstead Rifles loses four men killed on August 10, 1861, at the Battle of Oak Hills (Wilson's Creek) in Missouri. Afterward, the unit returns to Arkansas where it disbands, their three-month enlistment at an end. *Wilson's Creek National Battlefield, National Park Service*

The adventure soon turns into something more tedious, more difficult, and exceptionally deadly. Drilling is difficult, and the men find camp life boring. Diseases like measles, smallpox, and dysentery kills large numbers of men as they spread through camps of instruction. Following orders, something new to most of these young men—especially from former friends or family members, was also foreign to them.

The stunning Confederate victory along Bull Run creek on the plains of Manassas in north-central Virginia on July 21, 1861, does not end the war quickly—as so many believe it will. The victory disorganizes the raw Southern army nearly as much as the defeated Union command, and a march on Washington is simply not possible. On July 22, President Lincoln signs a bill providing for the enlistment of another 500,000 men for up to three years of service. Hopes for a quick victory fade.

Recruitment across the South lags as the reality of a long war sinks in. On January 22, 1862, the Confederate Congress approves a $50.00 bounty for men enlisting in the Confederate Army. That April, the Confederacy begins drafting men between the ages of 18 and 35.

They Called Him Johnny Reb

While every Confederate soldier had a name, more often than not he was Johnny Reb to the Yankees. Much like GI Joe in later wars, the moniker stuck. Sometimes his opponent, Bill Yank, called him Johnny or simply Reb. After the war many Confederates used the nickname with pride. Some even used the pen name "An Old Johnnie" when writing their autobiographies.

When war broke out in 1861, men flocked to enlist. Many enlisted for the thrill of it. They wanted to "see the elephant," another term for combat. The war gave them a chance for the adventure of their lives. A story or two to tell their grandchildren—if they survived. They had little connection to the national government and identified instead with their state. Most of the volunteers had never been out of their home state. The only Federal official most had encountered was a marshal who took the census every ten years.

While the official age for enlisting in the Confederate Army was 18, a number of boys skirted this requirement by enlisting as drummers or simply lying about their age. Birth certificates did not exist at that time, and few would-be recruits brought their family bible (in which was recorded such information) to enlist. Even a few women enlisted by claiming to be men. Physical examinations were rare and a number of females saw combat. For example, a Federal burial detail discovered the body of an unknown woman killed in Pickett's Charge at Gettysburg. African Americans had a more difficult time trying to disguise their race, but some enlisted in the Confederate Army despite regulations forbidding it.

The Federal Government kept good records of the men who enlisted in the Union Army, and most of these survive. Many Confederate records, however, were destroyed at the end of the war, or have been lost. However, a few

Private Ed Landvoigt of 1st Confederate Cavalry Regiment (left) and two unidentified soldiers in uniform, one with a sword. Landvoigt enlists in the Confederate Army at the first call for volunteers and serves throughout the war. He fights in many campaigns and battles including Shiloh, Fort Donelson, Murfreesboro (Stones River), Perryville, Lookout Mountain, the Atlanta Campaign, and at Fort Morgan at Mobile, Alabama, where his war ends when he is captured. *LOC*

generalizations can be made. The majority of Confederate enlisted men either owned their own farms or worked as a laborer on a farm. The largest city in the South was New Orleans, Louisiana, with a population of 161,044. The second-largest city was Charleston, South Carolina, with slightly more than 40,000. Florida, which had by far the smallest population of any Southern state, had almost five times as many cows as it did free whites. Most Southern towns, however, were smaller than 1,000 people, and most county seats had a population below 500.

Since most Confederate soldiers were farmers, they tended to be better marksmen than their Union counterparts, many of whom lived in towns and cities. Farmers and others who lived in rural areas, however, lived under very few rules and regulations in civilian life. As a result, the transition to military life proved difficult for many men.

Individual companies in the Confederate Army were normally composed of men from the same county. Quite often the company's unofficial name included the county or town from which the men originated, like the Cleveland Guards, Corinth Rifles, or the Claiborne Rangers.

Most of the men in the Confederate Army were born in the South. Many had heard stories about the American Revolution. They knew France had aided the colonists in their quest for independence. Even after the Union armies invaded the South, many Confederates clung to the belief that England and/or France would enter the war on the side of the South. Perhaps the soldiers' great-grandfathers' and uncles' stories of fighting at Kings Mountain and the Cowpens kept the hope of British intervention alive until the end.

A Soldier's Life

A soldier's life is almost entirely monotonous routine—the same boring thing every day without much relief—punctuated by short bursts of campaigning and battle that is often exhausting, terrifying, and deadly. Drill occupies hour after hour, as does guard duty or sitting in camp waiting for something to happen.

Confederate armies of 1861 are larger than anyone had ever witnessed before, and getting the men fed, clothed, properly housed, clean, and with proper medical attention is nearly impossible and a never-ending job.

In this 1861 photograph, a group of Confederates outside Pensacola, Florida, prepare for battle by drilling. *Photographic History of the Civil War*

Especially early in the war, one of the highlights of a soldier's day is mealtime. The mess of the Washington (Louisiana) Light Artillery is well-captured in this 1862 photo. Here, the unit is on garrison duty near Charleston, South Carolina. The wall tent behind them, as well as quality buckets, are rare luxuries for outfits engaged in active campaigning. *Photographic History of the Civil War*

Young soldiers meanwhile find themselves in camps of all sizes with friends, relatives, and officers from the same hometowns or vicinities. One of the most welcome things is getting a letter from home, and a favorite way to pass time is to pen a letter back to the loved ones. The new volunteers from across the South learn within days that soldier life is not as exciting as they had been led to believe. Each day offers more of the same of the previous day. As one solder described it, "We spend our time hunting up food or drilling or standing guard, and when not doing those things, all else maybe summed up in a word—waiting. We sit around and wait enough to drive one mad."

Most of the men can read at some level, so newspapers, letters, books, and Bibles help pass the time. Attending church or a religious ceremony is often welcome, as is playing games like chess, checkers, or cards. Some of the men gamble with dice or cards, or do other things they would never write about in a letter.

Regardless of what they do in camp, every new soldier regardless of his rank wonders whether he will be up to the challenge of battle—"seeing the

Confederate authorities use the young, partially disabled, and older men to guard prisons, hospitals, and supply depots so they can send able-bodied soldiers to the front lines. The young soldiers on the wall in this early-war photo are guarding Union prisoners at Castle Pinckney captured at First Manassas in July 1861. The small masonry fort is built in 1810 to guard, with other forts like Sumter, the important Charleston harbor in South Carolina. The fort proves too small and the prisoners are eventually transferred elsewhere. *LOC*

elephant." "Will I do my duty in battle?" is a concern on everyone's mind, as is, of course, "Will I be killed or horribly wounded?"

Camp life puts together thousands of men who had rarely, if ever, traveled more than 100 miles from their home. Hailing from a wide variety of backgrounds, from farmers and dry goods clerks to attorneys, bartenders,

(Above) Armies normally cease active campaigning during the winter months and settle into more substantial winter quarters. This Confederate camp is located near Centreville, Virginia. Note the quality of construction and the cleared streets. *LOC*

(Below) Rebel huts at Port Hudson, Louisiana, where Confederates garrisoning that important post on the Mississippi River live. *LOC*

This painting of a Confederate camp, published in England in 1871, is based on a drawing made by a sergeant in the 59th Virginia. *LOC*

students, and day laborers, they now shared the same tents, drill fields, and responsibilities.

Nearly every camp or command had some form of animal mascot. Usually they were dogs, but just about any domesticated animal would do. General Robert E. Lee kept a pet hen to provide him with fresh eggs.

The men of the Confederate 3rd Louisiana maintained a donkey that

Rev. Beverly Tucker Lacy is a chaplain and ardent Presbyterian from Fredericksburg, Virginia. Known widely as "Stonewall Jackson's Chaplain," Lacy plays a large role in the religious side of the war. Most Confederate soldiers are Protestants. Especially after the hard losses at Gettysburg and Vicksburg in the summer of 1863, religious services conducted by chaplains like Lacy play an important part of a soldier's life. *Photographic History of the Civil War*

(Left) Jonathan Sweet of Mississippi is shown here posing with a pistol and a bowie knife (which is nearly hidden on the opposite side). LOC

(Below) This unidentified member of the Richmond Howitzers is familiar with the pet gamecocks, and the camp and battle dog "Stonewall." LOC

wandered around camp and pushed open the colonel's tent under the mistaken belief he was his former owner.

Three companies that see long and bloody service in the war in the Eastern Theater (known as the Richmond Howitzers) keep pet gamecocks, and one of the companies keeps a dog named "Stonewall," after Gen. Thomas J. "Stonewall" Jackson. The small dog often rides inside a limber chest while on campaign and even attends roll calls, sitting in the line with its owners.

Surely the most unusual or exotic animal kept was the 43rd Mississippi Infantry's camel named "Douglas." It is a gift to Colonel W. H. Moore, but who gave it to him is something of a mystery. The camel carries the regimental bands instruments, and is eventually killed by a Union sharpshooter during the siege of Vicksburg on June 27, 1863.

(Above) Volunteers come to camp wearing a variety of clothing. Some of these soldiers appear to be wearing blue uniforms from their prewar militia units. *LOC*

(Below) Bivouac of Confederate troops on the Las Moras, Texas in March of 1861. Early in the war, US Army equipment, like this wagon, are liberated by Southern volunteers for Confederate use. *Photographic History of the Civil War*

Organization of the Confederate Armies

The Confederate Army's organization is modeled after the United States Army. Confederate leaders served in the United States Army and there is no time to experiment with other forms of organization.

The **company** is the building block of the Confederate Infantry. At the outbreak of the war companies have 100 officers and men. These men are recruited from the same town or county. At the beginning of the war the men in the company elect their own officers and noncommissioned officers. Most of the men in a company know each other and have a good idea of the company leaders' strengths. The company commander, a captain, is often the man who organized the company.

Infantry **regiments** consist of 10 companies designated by a letter. (There is no Company J because the letters I and J look very similar in the fancy manuscript of the day.) The companies in a regiment are from the same state but not from the same section of a state. Unlike the Union which recruits new regiments the Confederacy sends replacements to existing regiments. This practice gives raw recruits a chance to learn from experienced soldiers. As the war drags on fewer replacements are available, so some regiments are folded into other regiments to bring units up to strength.

Legions consist of infantry, cavalry, and artillery companies under a single commander. This command system proves impractical and legions are broken up and their companies are assigned to other units.

At the outbreak of the war, **brigades** are commanded by a brigadier general. As casualties mount, officers of a lesser rank often take command. Some of the famous brigades include the Stonewall Brigade, the Texas Brigade, and the Louisiana Brigade.

A **division** is the second largest unit in an army. A division is supposed to contain 8,000 to 12,000 soldiers, but the number in practice was much smaller. It is usually led by a brigadier or major general.

Patterned after the US Army (which in turn names them after the *corps d'armes* of the French Army), an infantry **corps** is usually composed of two or more divisions (a cavalry corps is similarly structured and includes various arms, but no infantry). A corps is usually commanded by a major or lieutenant general.

See the Organizational Chart (below) for more information:

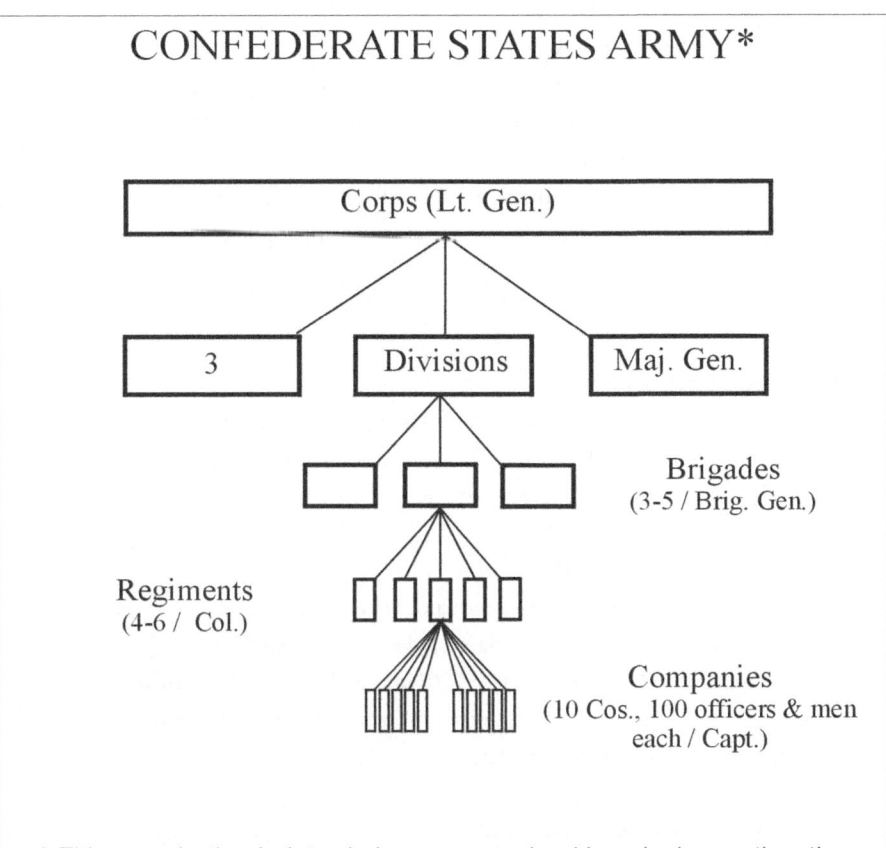

CONFEDERATE STATES ARMY*

Corps (Lt. Gen.)

3   Divisions   Maj. Gen.

Brigades
(3-5 / Brig. Gen.)

Regiments
(4-6 / Col.)

Companies
(10 Cos., 100 officers & men
each / Capt.)

* This organization is intended as a general guide only. In practice, the organization of armies and the ranks of commanders varied widely. For example, some corps had as few as two divisions, some divisions as few as two brigades, and many colonels commanded brigades in the field. These are but a few examples of how this structure varied in practice.

Most Confederate armies are named after states or geographic regions near which they operate—such as the Army of Northern Virginia or the Army of Tennessee. Some remain in the field for years, and others for just a short time. Below, in alphabetical order, are some of the most prominent Confederate armies created during the Civil War:

- **Army of Mississippi**
One of the most important Southern commands in the Western Theater and involved in several major battles including Shiloh, Corinth, and Perryville. It is known by different names, including Army of the West and Army of the Mississippi (which is what it was called at Shiloh). Organized in early March of 1862, elements of the Army of Pensacola arrive later that same month. It consolidates with the Army of Central Kentucky and the Army of Louisiana on March 29, 1862. On November 20, 1862, it is renamed the Army of Tennessee and will become the most important Confederate army of the Western Theater. Prominent commanders include Gens. P. G. T. Beauregard, Albert S. Johnston, and Braxton Bragg.

- **Army of Missouri**
This is an independent command within the Confederate Army created under Maj. Gen. Sterling Price in September 1864 to invade Missouri. Price's Raid is a failure, and his army is broken up that December.

- **Army of New Mexico**
This brigade-sized early-war command, also called the "Sibley Brigade," operates in Confederate Arizona and the New Mexico Territory during the New Mexico Campaign in late 1861 and early 1862. The campaign is a failure, and most of the men are transferred to serve in Louisiana. Its commander is Gen. Henry Sibley.

- **Army of Northern Virginia**
The primary command in the Eastern Theater for nearly the entire war. Unlike most armies, it is almost always pitted against the Union Army of the Potomac. Its origins go back to the Confederate Army of the Potomac (organized June 1861), with its name the informal consequence of the area in which it operates (northern Virginia). General Joseph E. Johnston is commanding the army when he is wounded on May 31, 1862, at Seven

Pines. General Robert E. Lee assumes command. Lee makes the army his own and famous, leading it until the end of the war in April 1865.

- **Army of the Valley**
  Officially designated Army of the Valley District, this independent command under Lt. Gen. Jubal Early is organized in the Shenandoah Valley to protect that vital area during the summer and fall of 1864. Early's command is the last to invade Northern soil and is famous for reaching the defenses on the outskirts of Washington. It is beaten several times and the Army, for all practical purposes, ceases to exist after its decisive defeat at the Battle of Waynesboro, Virginia, on March 2, 1865.

- **Army of the South**
  This field army exists during the final months of the war, created out of several Confederate commands during the campaign in the Carolinas. It fights in one major battle (Bentonville, March 1865), reorganizes as the Army of Tennessee, and surrenders at the end of April 1865.

- **Army of Tennessee**
  Like the Army of Northern Virginia in the Eastern Theater, this command is the principal army of the Western Theater (defined as the Appalachian Mountains on the east and the Mississippi River on the west). It is formed out of the Army of Mississippi in late 1862 and fights until the surrender in 1865 in almost all of the major battles in that theater. Its primary commanders are Gens. Braxton Bragg and Joseph E. Johnston.

There are other important organizations, without which armies cannot function. The Quartermaster Department takes care of field equipment, shelter, and transport, while the Commissary handles food and animal fodder, and the Ordnance Department weapons, such as cannon, muskets, and ammunition.

Campaigning armies are almost always followed by long and cumbersome wagon trains full of supplies and equipment.

A Concise Timeline of the American Civil War

Many battles were called by different names. Confederates tended to name battles after the nearest town or city. The Union normally named battles after nearby rivers or creeks. Thus, the battle fought around the small town of Sharpsburg, Maryland, on September 17, 1862, was known in the South as Sharpsburg, and in the North as Antietam (after a creek coursing through the battlefield). In the list that follows, the Confederate name is used first, while the Union name is provided in parentheses.

1860
November 6: Abraham Lincoln is elected as the 16th president of the United States.

December 17: Secession Convention meets in Columbia, South Carolina.

December 20: South Carolina secedes from the Union.

1861
January: Mississippi, Florida, Alabama, Georgia, Louisiana, and Texas secede from the Union.

February 8-9: Confederacy forms at Montgomery, Alabama.

February 18: Jefferson Davis is elected president of the Confederate States of America.

April 12: Southern forces fire on Fort Sumter at Charleston, South Carolina.

June 10: Confederates win the Battle of Big Bethel, the first land battle of the war in Virginia.

July 21: Union Army routed at First Battle of Manassas (Bull Run) in Virginia.

August 10: Confederate victory at Oak Hill (Wilson's Creek), in Missouri.

August 28-29: Fort Hatteras in North Carolina falls to Union naval forces.

September 20: Lexington, Missouri, falls to Confederate forces.

October 21: Battle of Ball's Bluff in Virginia. The bodies of many of the Union soldiers who are killed or drown float down the Potomac River to Washington.

1862

January 19: Confederates repulsed at Logan's Cross-Roads (Mill Springs) Kentucky.

February 6: Confederates surrender of Fort Henry in Tennessee.

February 8: Roanoke Island, North Carolina, falls to Federal troops.

February 16: Confederates surrender of Fort Donelson in Tennessee.

March-June: Thomas "Stonewall" Jackson fights and defeats three Union Armies in Virginia's Shenandoah Valley.

March 7-8: Union victory at Elkhorn Tavern (Pea Ridge) in Arkansas.

March 9: The ironclads USS *Monitor* and CSS *Virginia* fight a history-making battle to a draw at Hampton Roads, Virginia.

April 6-7: Union victory at Shiloh (Pittsburg Landing), Tennessee.

April 24-25: Union Navy captures New Orleans.

May 31-June 1: Battle of Seven Pines (Fair Oaks) near Richmond, Virginia.

June 6: Memphis, Tennessee, falls to Union Naval forces.

June 25-July 1: Confederates drive Union troops away from Richmond in the Seven Days' Battles.

August 28-30: Confederates win the Second Battle of Manassas (Bull Run) in Virginia.

September 17: Battle of Sharpsburg (Antietam) ends Robert E. Lee's invasion of Maryland.

October 3-4: Confederate attempt to retake Corinth, Mississippi, repulsed.

October 8: The Battle of Perryville ends Bragg's Invasion of Kentucky.

December 13: Federals repulsed in the Battle of Fredericksburg, Virginia.

December 31-January 3, 1863: Confederates fight and lose the Battle of Murfreesboro (Stones River) in Tennessee.

1863

January 1: Emancipation Proclamation takes effect.

May 1-4: Confederates win the Battle of Chancellorsville, Virginia. Confederate General Thomas "Stonewall" Jackson is mortally wounded by friendly fire.

May 16: Union victory at Champion Hill (Baker's Creek) in Mississippi dooms Vicksburg. Grant besieges Vicksburg two days later.

June 9: The largest cavalry battle of is fought at Brandy Station, Virginia.

June 14-15: Confederates win the Second Battle of Winchester, Virginia.

July 1-3: Confederates defeated at Gettysburg, Pennsylvania.

July 4: Vicksburg, Mississippi, surrenders to Maj. Gen. Ulysses S. Grant.

July 9: Port Hudson, Louisiana, surrenders after a 58-day siege. The Mississippi River is open for shipping.

July 13: Draft Riots begin in New York City.

July 18: Second assault on Battery Wagner, South Carolina, fails.

September 9: Union troops occupy Chattanooga, Tennessee.

September 18-20: Confederates win the Battle of Chickamauga, Georgia.

September–November 1863: Confederates besiege Chattanooga.

November 19: Abraham Lincoln gives a brief speech at Gettysburg.

November 24-25: Battles of Lookout Mountain and Missionary Ridge break the Confederate siege of Chattanooga.

November 26-December 1: Union Mine Run campaign fails.

November 27-December 3: Confederate siege of Knoxville, Tennessee, fails.

1864

February 27: Andersonville prison camp is opened in Georgia.

February 14-20: Union forces capture Meridian, Mississippi.

February 17: The submersible *H. L. Hunley* sinks the USS *Houstonic* outside Charleston, South Carolina, in the first successful submarine attack in history.

March 3: Ulysses S. Grant assumes command of all Union forces.

March 10: Red River campaign begins in Louisiana.

April 8-9: The battles of Mansfield (Sabine Crossroads) and Pleasant Hill, Louisiana, end the Red River campaign.

April 12: Confederates capture of Fort Pillow in Tennessee.

May 4-5: Battle of the Wilderness in Virginia.

May 8-21: Battles around Spotsylvania Court House in Virginia.

May 11: Confederate cavalry commander Maj. Gen. James E. B. Stuart is mortally wounded in the Battle of Yellow Tavern in Virginia.

May 14-15: Indecisive Battle of Resaca (Lay's Ferry) in Georgia.

May 15: Cadets from the Virginia Military Institute fight in the Confederate victory New Market, Virginia.

June 1-3: Union attack repulsed at Cold Harbor in Virginia.

June 10: Federals defeated at Brice's Cross Roads (Tishomingo Creek), Mississippi.

June 15-18: Union assault on Petersburg, Virginia, fails. A nine month siege begins.

June 19: The USS *Kearsarge* sinks the Confederate raider CSS *Alabama* off Cherbourg, France.

June 27: Union assult at Kennesaw Mountain, Georgia, fails.

July 9: Union delaying action at Monocacy, Maryland, saves Washington from invading Confederates.

July 11-12: Confederates probe the defenses of Washington, D.C.

July 14-15: Confederates defeated at Tupelo, Mississippi.

July 20: Confederate attack repulsed at Peachtree Creek near Atlanta,

July 22: Federals defeat Confederates in the Atlanta.

July 30: Confederates win the Battle of the Crater near Petersburg.

August 5: Union Navy wins the Battle of Mobile Bay, Alabama.

August 18-19: Union troops fail in their effort to cut the Weldon Railroad south of Petersburg, Virginia.

August 25: Confederates capture over 2,100 Federals in the Battle of Ream's Station, near Petersburg, Virginia

August 31-September 1, 1864: Union victory at Jonesborough, near Atlanta.

September 2: Fall of Atlanta.

September 19: Confederates defeated in the Third Battle of Winchester, Virginia.

September 22: Union victory at Fisher's Hill, in Virginia.

September 29-30: Federals capture Fort Harrison near Richmond.

October 19: Federals win the Battle of Belle Grove (Cedar Creek), in Virginia.

November 8: Lincoln is reelected president of the United States.

November 16: General Sherman begins his "March to the Sea."

November 30: Confederate attack repulsed in the Battle of Franklin, Tennessee.

December 10: Sherman's army group arrives at Savannah, Georgia, completing the "March to the Sea."

December 15-16: Union victory at Nashville in Tennessee.

1865

January 15: Federal troops capture Fort Fisher in North Carolina.

February 1: Sherman's command leaves Savannah to march through the Carolinas.

February 17: Columbia, South Carolina, captured.

February 22: Wilmington, North Carolina, falls to Union troops.

March 11: Sherman occupies Fayetteville, North Carolina.

March 16, and 19-21: Battles of Averasboro and Bentonville in North Carolina.

March 25: Confederate attack against Fort Stedman fails at Petersburg.

April 1: Union victory at Five Forks, Virginia.

April 2: The Army of Northern Virginia evacuates Richmond and Petersburg.

April 3: Union troops occupy Richmond and Petersburg.

April 6: Union victory at Sailor's Creek, in Virginia.

April 9: Lee surrenders the Army of Northern Virginia at Appomattox Court House, Virginia.

April 12: The Army of Northern Virginia is formally disbanded.

April 14: Lincoln assassinated by actor John Wilkes Booth.

April 14: Fort Sumter in South Carolina is reoccupied by Union troops.

April 26: The Confederate Army of Tennessee surrenders near Durham, North Carolina.

May 4: General Richard Taylor surrenders Confederate forces in the Department of Alabama, Mississippi, and East Louisiana.

May 10: Confederate President Jefferson Davis is captured near Irwinville, Georgia.

May 12: The final battle of the Civil War, a small Confederate victory, takes place at Palmito Ranch, Texas.

June 23: The last major Confederate force to surrender is led by Cherokee General Stand Watie, who stands down with his Indian soldiers.

November 6: The raider CSS *Shenandoah* surrenders at Liverpool, England.

Numbers and Losses

The chart that follows on the next page includes figures for both Union and Confederate forces. Because many Confederate documents were lost at the end of the war, the figures provided for Southern forces are estimates based on the most complete data available.

Federal soldiers enlisted for a specified length of time, while Confederates who did so enlisted for the duration of the war. An unknown number of Federal soldiers enlisted in different units after their original enlistment expired.

Most of the troops who were wounded, but not mortally so, returned to their units or were assigned to other commands. Union soldiers too disabled to return to their front-line units were often transferred to the Veteran Reserve Corps. These soldiers guarded supply depots and prison camps, which freed able-bodied soldiers for front-line duty. Wounded Confederates were often detailed for similar duties.

Many Union soldiers enlisted to receive a bounty paid to volunteers. These bounties range from $300.00 to as high as $700.00. "Bounty Jumpers" are men who enlist to collect the money, only to desert at the first opportunity and repeat the process over and over. Some "Bounty Jumpers" joined as many as half-a- dozen units during the course of the war.

At least 21,000 Confederate deserters were captured and returned to duty. Soldiers who were discharged when their enlistment expired are not included in this figure dealing with discharges.

	UNION	CONFEDERATE
Total Number of Enlistments	2,772,408	1,000,000
Killed in Battle	67,058	53,000
Mortally Wounded	40,940	30,000
Died of Disease	199,720	100,000
Killed in Accidents	4,071	3,000
Drowned	4,937	3,500
Died of Other Known Causes	3,362	2,500
Died of Unknown Causes	10,082	...
Died while a Prisoner of War	25,971	27,000
Total Deaths	356,141	219,000
Wounded in Action (not mortally)	275,000	226,000
Captured	211,400	287,777
Deserted	199,000	104,000
Discharged	426,500	57,800
Surrendered in 1865		174,223

Unfortunately, no accurate data for the Confederate army exists because of poor record-keeping and lost or destroyed records. Depending upon the source, estimates of how many men served in gray at any time during the war range from as low as 500,000 to as high as 2,000,000. The earliest report from the Confederate War Department was issued at the end of 1861 showing 326,768 men under arms, followed by another in 1862 (449,439), 1863 (464,646), 1864 (400,787), and "last reports" (358,692). The best estimates of enlistments throughout the war are 1,227,890 to 1,406,180.

Photography

The Civil War is the first war in history to be widely photographed. More than 1,000 photographers worked during the conflict, though most have passed into history unidentified.

Producing a single photograph is quite a process. Two photographers are usually required to capture a picture. It is especially difficult to work from a photography wagon on a battlefield. One photographer prepares clean glass

The Civil War was the first to be widely photographed. Photographs were shot using a "wet plate" process. Glass plates were treated with collodion and silver nitrate before being exposed for several seconds. The glass was then developed in a darkroom. The mobile darkroom in the photo above was taken at Manassas Battlefield. *LOC*

A camp at Petersburg, Virginia. Glass plates are fragile, as the photograph above shows. *Photographic History of the Civil War*

plates and the chemicals needed, which he pours onto the plate. After some time for the chemicals to evaporate, the plate is immersed in a bath solution and placed in a holder. This process is done in complete darkness.

To use the plate, the photographer inserts the holder into the camera, which is positioned by the other photographer. Exposure of the plate—usually several seconds—and development of the photograph has to be completed within minutes. Each exposed plate is rushed to the darkroom wagon for developing. The resulting glass plate negative is very fragile.

Photography also made something else possible. In addition to capturing the likenesses of tens of thousands of young men for family members back home to see, the men behind the cameras also captured photographs of the dead, something that had never been done before.

Often new recruits had their photographs taken in their new uniform at photography studios like this one at Corinth, Mississippi. Southern photographers had to purchase chemicals from either Northern or European chemical companies. As the war progressed and the Union naval blockade tightened the supply of photographic chemical dried up. *LOC*

Like so many photographs that have survived, the name of the young Confederate soldier (right) has been lost to history. He has a small book in pocket, which is likely a Bible. *LOC*

Soldiers often send their photograph home to their mothers, wives, or girlfriends. Loved ones treasure these images. Unfortunately, the identities of many Civil War soldiers and sailors in these photographs have been lost or forgotten. The two photographs above and on the facing page are in the same case. The young ladies are named Mollie Knopp Zigler (left) and Betty Hoover (right). The Confederate navy midshipman on the facing page, however, is unidentified, so their relationship remains a mystery. Perhaps they are brother and sisters, or one of the women was the midshipman's wife or girlfriend? In all likelihood, we shall never know. *LOC*

Weapons of War

The war is a showcase for different weapons. It witnesses the use of edged weapons (knives to swords) and pistols, rifles, muskets, and even repeating weapons. Rifled gun barrels rule the day and make the Minie ball (see next page) especially deadly, and the explosive variety deadlier still.

The Minie Ball combined with the rifled musket gives soldiers in defensive positions a tremendous advantage against attacking troops. Earlier wars, including the American Revolution and the Mexican War, were fought with smoothbore muskets with a maximum effective range of about 50 yards. Soldiers armed with the smoothbore muskets lined up and exchanged volleys of fire until one side either broke and ran, or attacked with the bayonet. The attackers had an advanatage and usually won the battle. The increased range of

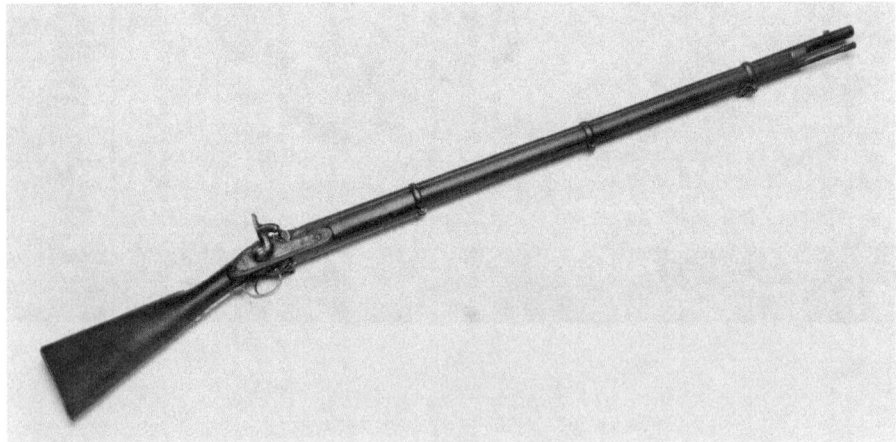

Enfield Rifled Musket. Faced with an overwhelming demand for small arms, the Confederacy imports hundreds of thousands of rifled muskets. The most popular is the English Enfield rifled musket (Pattern 1853). It weighs 9.5 pounds, measures 55 inches long with a 39-inch barrel, and fires a .58 caliber bullet up to 1,000 yards. A trained soldier can fire his Enfield three times in one minute. *North Carolina Museum of History*

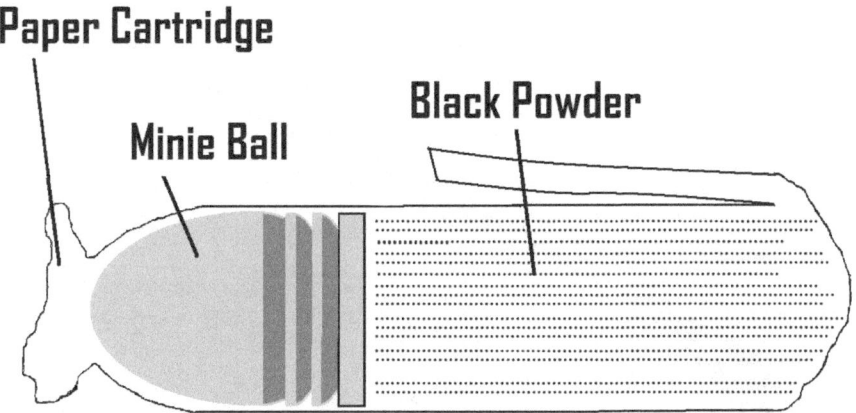

Paper Cartridge
Minie Ball
Black Powder

Both the Enfield (previous page) and Springfield (next page) rifled muskets fire a lead projectile known as a "Minié" ball, named after its inventor and French army captain Claude-Etienne Minié. Soldiers carry Minie Balls in paper or linen cartridges that contain a black powder charge (above). To load a rifled musket, the soldier tears the powder end of the cartridge and pours the powder down the barrel. He inserts the Minié ball, pointed end up, and uses his ramrod to shove it down the barrel. When fired, the hollow base of the bullet expands to grip the barrel's rifling, spinning the lead round as it exits the weapon. The spin provides increased speed, range, and accuracy. *Author*

the rifled musket, however, makes a frontal assault a costly tactic that usually fails.

At the beginning of the war, state militia units seize many Federal forts in the South. Even with the weapons taken from these forts, militia armories, and the Federal arsenal at Harpers Ferry, Virginia, the Confederacy faces shortages

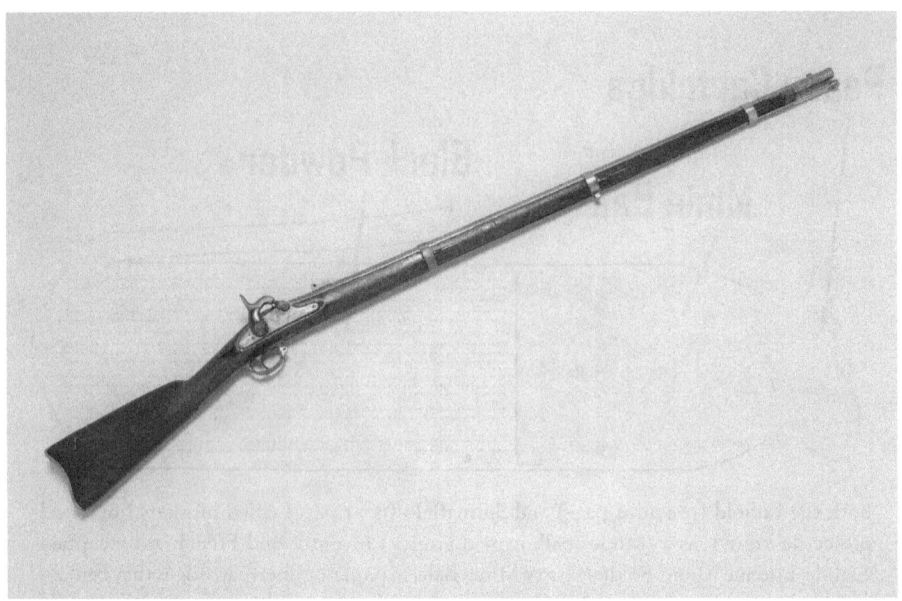

Springfield 1861 Rifled Musket (Model 1861). The most widely used weapon of the war. Northern factories produce hundreds of thousands of this .58 caliber weapon. The weapon is half a pound lighter than the Enfield with the same range and rate of fire. Confederates capture and use thousands of Springfields. *North Carolina Museum of History*

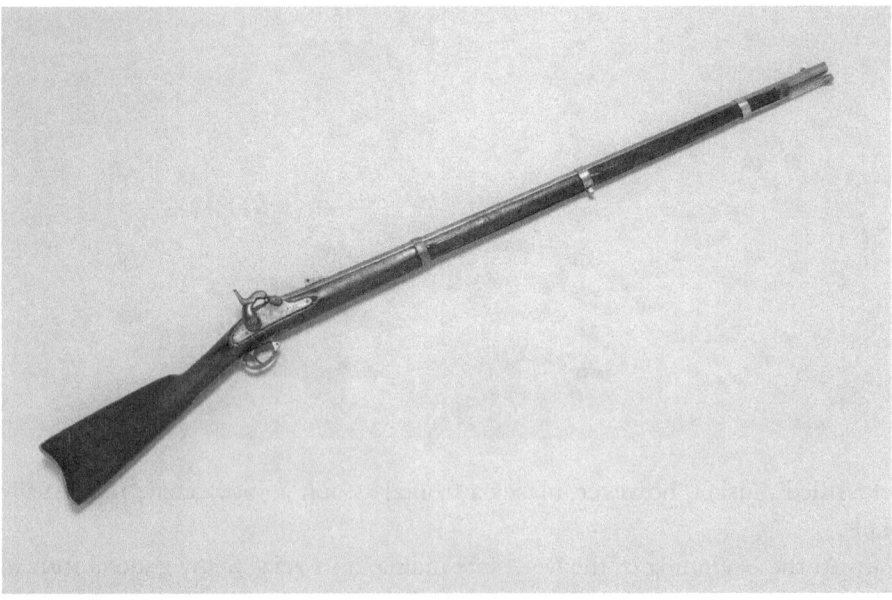

Fayetteville Rifled Musket. Confederates capture the U.S. Arsenal at Harpers Ferry, Virginia, move the machinery to Fayetteville, North Carolina, and produce small arms. This version is similar to the Springfield. *North Carolina Museum of History*

A 10-inch Columbiad and magazine entrance. Heavy Columbiad cannons are often mounted in forts to command ocean or river defenses. This 10-inch gun weighs more than 15,000 pounds and fires a 128-lb. shell nearly 5,000 yards. This piece is at Battery Dantzler on the James River between Petersburg and Richmond. *Photographic History of the Civil War*

of both small arms and artillery. Northern armies are also short of weapons, and both sides work to train armies, so little fighting occurs in 1861.

On the explosive side of the ledger, torpedoes—stationary explosives just under the surface of the water usually set off with an electric charge—are used to sink enemy ships. Land mines were also introduced, though many on both sides consider them to be dishonorable. A different kind of underground explosive is employed outside Petersburg in July 1864 in the Battle of the Crater, where Union troops set off a giant mine under the Confederate lines. Even hand grenades were tossed about in close quarters, seeing use in many campaigns including Vicksburg and the long Petersburg siege.

Like many conflicts throughout history, 1861-1865 proves a rich environment of invention for the killing implements of war.

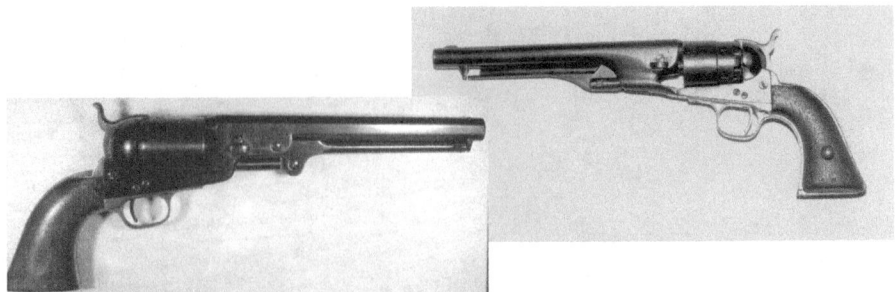

Arguably the most common sidearm of the Civil War, the .36 caliber Colt 1851 "Navy" revolver (top left), a six-shot, muzzle-loading pistol used by soldiers and sailors on both sides. Colt's .44 caliber 1860 "Army" revolver (top right) is also popular. *United States Army, Rock Island Arsenal Museum, Rock Island, Illinois*

English Armstrong gun. Almost all Civil War cannon are muzzle- loaders. Artillerymen pack black powder and shells into the front (muzzle) of the cannon. The Confederacy imports a small number of breech-loading Armstrong guns from England. This piece is installed at Fort Fisher, North Carolina. *LOC*

Always in the need of more guns, the Confederates employ logs painted black to look like cannons. Although not a real weapon, from a distance the enemy believed it was an artillery piece. This "Quaker Gun" is mounted at Centreville, Virginia. The soldier is pretending to light its fuse for the photographer. *LOC*

This 12-lb. bronze Napoleon gun was the most popular of the war on both sides. It was designed for field use, and was highly versatile. Here, Union men from Sherman's army pose with a captured piece in one of the forts ringing Atlanta, Georgia. *LOC*

Battles and Battlefields

At the outset of the war Southern leaders are content to block Union advances and wait for Northern citizens to demand an end to the war.

During the early months of the conflict, Northern strategy is simple. Many believe the war will end with the capture of the Confederate capital, so the war cry in the North is "On to Richmond!" The first Union attempt to take the city fails with the Confederate victory at First Manassas in July 1861. Other larger

Inexperienced soldiers fight the first major battle of the war at Manassas, Virginia, on July 21, 1861. Although the Confederates win what they call First Manassas (or, First Bull Run in the North), they were unable to pursue the beaten Yankees. Confederate General P. G. T. Beauregard used Wilmer McLean's home as his headquarters. (The photo above is usually depicted as the McLean house, though it has also been identified as the Weir family home called "Liberia.") Tired of the young war, McLean moved south to Appomattox Court House, Virginia. On April 9, 1865, Confederate General Robert E. Lee surrendered to General U. S. Grant in McLean's parlor. *LOC*

On August 10, 1861, Confederates defeat Union forces at the Battle of Oak Hills (Wilson's Creek) in a critically important combat in southwestern Missouri. This view of the field looks northeast from what is known as "Bloody Hilly." Despite the battlefield victory, the Southern army once more fails to pursue the defeated Federals. Northern Missouri remains in the Union. *Wilson's Creek National Battlefield*

campaign efforts ensue, including: The Seven Days' Battles (June-July 1862), Second Manassas (August 1862), Fredericksburg (December 1862), and Chancellorsville (April-May 1863). In 1864, General Ulysses S. Grant changes the objective to Robert E. Lee's Army of Northern Virginia. A bloody series of battles from The Wilderness, Spotsylvania, and Cold Harbor (May-June 1864) take the armies south to James River, which Grant crosses to reach Petersburg and Richmond, which he fails to immediately capture.

In the Western Theater, the Union uses rivers to move troops and supplies south and scores victories at Forts Henry and Donelson (February 1862), and

(Above) Union General George B. McClellan moves troops to the Virginia peninsula by ship in March 1862. General Joseph E. Johnston's Confederates use fortifications and difficult terrain to bog him down for weeks around Yorktown before finally retreating toward Richmond. McClellan follows and just miles outside the Southern capital Johnston attacks him at Seven Pines (Fair Oaks) on May 31-June 1, 1862. This view is the rear of an old frame house, orchard, and well at Seven Pines. More than 400 soldiers are buried here after the battle. (Below) Robert E. Lee's tactical victory during the Seven Days' Battles at Gaines' Mill near Richmond on June 27, 1862, prompts McClellan to retreat to the James River and abandon his plans to capture Richmond. *LOC*

Shiloh (April 1862). Control of the Mississippi River greatly assists the long but successful sieges of Vicksburg (May-July 1863) and Port Hudson (May-July 1863), and completely open the river to Union shipping.

A Federal victory at Murfreesboro (Stones River) at the end of 1862/early 1863 opens Middle Tennessee to Union occupation. Confederates turn back the first Union push into Georgia at Chickamauga (September 1863), but Federals break the Confederate siege of Chattanooga that follows (September-November 1863) that leaves Georgia open to invasion. General Sherman moves south in May 1864 and Atlanta falls that September.

In the Trans-Mississippi Theater, Confederates squander an early victory at Oak Hills (Wilson's Creek) in southwestern Missouri (August 1861), and a major Federal victory at Elkhorn Tavern (Pea Ridge) (March 1862) secures Missouri and northern Arkansas for the Union.

The Confederates launch three significant invasions of the North, and each fails: Sharpsburg (September 1862), Perryville (October 1862), and Gettysburg (July 1863).

In August 1862 the Union and Confederate armies met again on the Manassas battlefield. Just as they had in the first battle there, the Confederates prevail at Second Manassas (August 28-29, 1862) and rout the enemy back to Washington. The famous "Stone House" pictured here at the intersection of the Warrenton Turnpike (modern US 29) and Sudley Road (Va 234) served as a field hospital and was a prominent landmark during the fighting. *LOC*

(Above) After defeating the Union Army at Second Manassas, General Lee invades Maryland. Troops under General Thomas "Stonewall" Jackson capture Harpers Ferry, in western Virginia, on September 15, 1862, which is pictured here. (Below) Lee's first invasion of the North ends at the Battle of Sharpsburg (Antietam) Maryland on September 17, 1862. More than 23,000 men from both sides, including these Louisiana troops, who died along the Hagerstown Road, were killed, wounded, or captured in the bloodiest one-day battle in American history. *LOC*

(Above) The "Rohrbach's" or "lower" bridge, looking across Antietam Creek toward the western bank. The structure is best known as "Burnside's Bridge" after Ambrose Burnside, the Union corps commander who spent hours trying to cross it in the face of stubborn resistance from 500 Rebel defenders under General Robert Toombs, who held the high ground. (Below) The last phase of the Sharpsburg fighting began hours after Burnside crossed the river with an attack by his IX Corps that reached the vicinity of the town itself. Luckily for the Confederates, A. P. Hill's division reaches the field after a long march from Harpers Ferry and counterattacks near the Lutheran church, pictured here, and throws back the assault. *LOC*

(Above) On December 13, 1862, the Confederate Army of Northern Virginia repulsed repeated assaults on both ends of their line west of Fredericksburg, Virginia, seen here from the eastern side of the Rappahannock River. General Burnside's Army of the Potomac lost more than 12,000 men killed, wounded, and captured, while the Confederates lost fewer than half that number. LOC (Below) On Sunday, April 6, 1862, Gen. Albert S. Johnston launches a surprise attack and shoves back the Federals under Maj. Gen. Ulysses S. Grant near Shiloh Church, Tennessee. A determined defensive effort (including along the Sunken Road, gunfire from Union warships at Pittsburg Landing on the Tennessee River, poor Southern command decisions, and the death of Johnston), help Grant's army stave off destruction. Reinforced that night, Grant attacks the next day and drives the Confederates off the field. *Shiloh National Military Park*

(Above) Civilians stand outside the train station at the strategic railroad junction of Corinth, Mississippi. In early October 1862 Confederates tried to retake the town, but were repulsed with heavy losses. (Below) At Chancellorsville, Virginia, in early May 1863, General Lee divides his army and outgenerals Union Major General "Fighting Joe" Hooker. Near these trees shattered by artillery fire, Major General Thomas J. "Stonewall" Jackson was mortally wounded by friendly fire. LOC

(Above) Robert E. Lee's second invasion of the North ended in the war's largest battle at the small town of Gettysburg, Pennsylvania, shown here in this photo. Lee's army caught General Meade's Army of the Potomac moving quickly up from the south, and defeated two of its corps west and north of town on July 1, 1863. (Below) Culp's Hill, a major Confederate objective on July 2 at Gettysburg, remained in Union hands despite repeated costly Confederate attacks to take it. The Confederates briefly captured part of East Cemetery Hill (at the bottom of the photo) at dusk, but were driven off. *LOC*

(Above) Part of the Confederate attack at Gettysburg late on the afternoon of July 2 pushed into the Devil's Den, a boulder-strewn area below Little Round Top. The Confederates had no idea the terrain was so bad, and coupled with a strong Union defensive effort, prevented the collapse of the left flank of Meade's army. Here a dead Southern soldier lies near a rifled musket, placed there as a prop by a photographer after the battle. (Below) Late on July 2 at Gettysburg, thousands of men from both sides marched into the Wheatfield, a 20-acre area bordered by the Rose Woods and Stony Hill. The land changes hands several times. Nearly 21,000 men fight there and about 30% are killed, wounded, or captured. By nightfall, the land is firmly in Union hands. *LOC*

(Above) The Confederates lost more than 27,000 men killed, wounded, or missing at Gettysburg, and the Union about 23,000. Handling the dead is a gruesome task left to the victor of the field. The vast majority are gathered for burial close to where they fell. In 1872, most of the Confederates are removed and buried in Richmond's Hollywood Cemetery. These Confederate dead, about 15 men from George Anderson's brigade on the Rose farm, fell late on the afternoon of July 2. (Below) Hasty wooden headboards mark the unfinished graves of what appear to be four Confederates semi-buried near the center of the battlefield at Gettysburg. *LOC*

(Above) Confederates turned back several attempts at Holly Springs and elsewhere by Union Maj. Gen. U. S. Grant to reach Vicksburg, Mississippi, from the north. Grant used several inland diversions to confuse Southern commander John C. Pemberton (whose headquarters are pictured here) and marched his Army of the Tennessee down the Louisiana side of the river and crossed below the city at the end of April 1863 without opposition. (Below) The strong Confederate batteries at Vicksburg were unable to keep Union warships and troopships from passing south down the Mississippi River, which made it possible for them to protect Grant's crossing below the city. Pictured here is the Vicksburg waterfront and the broad river. *LOC*

(Above) After defeating the Federals at Chickamauga on September 18-20, 1863, Confederate General Braxton Bragg's Army of Tennessee pursued Maj. Gen. William Rosecrans's battered Army of the Cumberland to Chattanooga, Tennessee, which he partially surrounds. Confederates hold strong positions on Lookout Mountain and Missionary Ridge. Chattanooga was a major river and manufacturing center and logistical hub. This view shows artillery on Lookout Mountain overlooking the winding Tennessee River and Chattanooga. (Below) Major General U. S. Grant assumed Union command and captured Lookout Mountain on November 24, 1863, in what is known as "The Battle above the Clouds." The Cravens house (below) was about halfway up the slope and a key fixture in the fight. The next day, Union men capture Missionary Ridge and drive the Rebels into North Georgia in a stunning defeat. *LOC*

After his string of victories in the Western Theater, Maj. Gen. U. S. Grant was promoted to lead all the Federal armies. He made his headquarters with Meade's Army of the Potomac and organized a coordinated attack against the Confederacy in the Spring of 1864. He moved south across the Rapidan River against Lee's Army of Northern Virginia in early May, triggering the Battle of the Wilderness (May 5-7), where more than 150,000 soldiers fought in the tangled terrain west of Fredericksburg. This photograph shows Confederate breastworks on the battlefield. *LOC*

(Above) Instead of retreating after the fierce stalemate fighting in the Wilderness, Grant moves around Lee's right flank and the armies meet again at Spotsylvania Court House. There, they erect miles of earthworks and lock bayonets in a twelve-day bloodbath that inflicts 13,000 Confederate losses and more than 18,000 Union. Grant launches several assaults against the Confederate lines, including a massive dawn attack on May 12 against the "Muleshoe," breaks Lee's center, and nearly severs his army. Here, a Rebel soldier lies dead, killed in the Harris Farm fighting on May 19. (Below) Major General William T. Sherman, meanwhile, leads three Union armies south into Georgia against Gen. J. E. Johnston's Army of Tennessee. The campaign of maneuver and fighting drives deep into Georgia. Sherman is sharply repulsed at Kennesaw Mountain on June 27, 1864. *LOC*

After Kennesaw, Sherman outflanks Johnston, crosses the Chattahoochee River, and triggers major fighting around Atlanta, including the battles of Peachtree Creek (July 20), Atlanta (July 22), and Ezra Church (July 28). (Above) Confederate fortifications on Atlanta's northwest side include the heavily damaged Ephraim Ponder house, which is pounded by Union artillery. (Below) Fortifications and trenches around Petersburg. *LOC*

(Above) After losing Atlanta, Gen. John Bell Hood eventually led his Confederate Army of Tennessee into the state of Tennessee. He nearly blocked and captured Maj. Gen. John Scofield's Army of the Ohio at Spring Hill on November 28, 1864. The next day, with Scofield up against the Harpeth River, Hood launched a massive attack at Franklin. He was repulsed with heavy losses. Hood continued north and took up a position outside Nashville, where a reinforced Union command under Maj. Gen. George Thomas attacked and defeated him on December 15-16 in one of the most complete victories of the war. The image here shows the outer Union line in the Nashville battlefield. (Below) One of the most important Southern seaports was Wilmington, North Carolina, which was protected for years by the massive Fort Fisher. A combined Union naval and land attack in early January 1865 doomed the bastion, which fell on the 15th. LOC

Technology and the Civil War

Technology advances rapidly during the war with many "firsts," including railroads to move troops, land mines, ironclad ships, submarines, hot-air balloons, and much more. Major advances are made in medicine, caring for the wounded, and nursing.

Perhaps the most important development—together with the rifled musket discussed earlier—is the first widespread use of railroads to move troops and supplies.

The Tredegar Iron Works in Richmond, Virginia, is the largest and most important privately owned manufacturing facility in the Confederacy. The facility produces more than 1,000 artillery pieces, plating for ironclads, locomotives, and even parts for Confederate submarines. It is indispensable for Southern war effort. The Richmond National Battlefield's main visitor center occupies the site today. *LOC*

The signal system is an American device first tested in warfare against hostile Navajos. Both Federal and Confederate armies improve on the idea in significant ways and use portable signaling throughout the war. Signal towers are one way to send messages. This Confederate lookout tower above is at Bolivar Point, Texas. Note the man on top of the tower.

The signal tower below is near Fort McAllister, Georgia, and guards the land approach to Savannah until Sherman's army captures it in December 1864. *LOC*

The Civil War sees the first widespread use of railroads to move troops and supplies over long distances. At the outbreak of the war some 100 Southern railroad companies have 9,500 miles of track in operation. This photo of Atlanta's massive railroad yard is made before it was destroyed in 1864. LOC

In 1861 there are about 100 Southern railroad companies using 9,500 miles of track to move agricultural products like cotton to market or to river or coastal ports. Most of these private railroads do not connect to other lines, and use a variety of gauges that made it difficult for train cars on one railroad to use another. Despite these drawbacks, Confederates make good use of railroads to transport troops, supplies, the wounded and the sick soldiers, and prisoners.

These pages include photos and information on some of the South's most significant technological achievements of the Civil War.

The Augusta Powderworks (below, with the Augusta canal in the foreground) is the brainchild of Maj. George Washington Rains (inset, immediate postwar view). President Jefferson Davis tasks Rains in the summer of 1861 to find the perfect location to erect a powder mill "of sufficient magnitude" to supply the Confederacy with its wartime needs. Rains designs and erects the giant facility just outside Augusta, Georgia, and has it running by April 1862. He develops a host of technologically advanced buildings and machinery designs, and uses his chemistry background to produce what is universally hailed as the finest gunpowder in the world. The facility is so valuable that its destruction would have ended the war within a few months. It operates until the end of April 1865. *LOC*

Unable to compete with Union shipbuilding, Confederate Secretary of the Navy Stephen Mallory decides to construct ironclad ships. The sloping casemate design is very recognizable, and proves itself in many engagements. Although these ships are not as successful as he hopes, they play a much larger role in the war than many people believe by blocking rivers, protecting harbors, and acting as giant floating batteries. Shown here are the CSS *Chicora* (top) and the CSS *Atlanta* (bottom) after its capture off Savannah, Georgia. The *Chicora's* interesting career includes (with the CSS *Palmetto State*) a sea battle outside the entrance of Charleston harbor against Federal blockaders. Thereafter, and mostly from positions at anchor, she defends the forts guarding Charleston against enemy ironclad monitors. Confederates destroy the *Chicora* in February 1865 as they evacuate the city. The CSS *Atlanta's* career is much shorter and disastrous. The ironclad is constructed from the converted steamer SS *Fingal* in November 1862. In June 1863, she steams out to attack Federal warships blockading the coast, grounds on a sandbar, and is pounded into submission and surrenders to the USS *Weehawken*. She is renamed USS *Atlanta* and serves the Union navy until the end of the war. *LOC*

The Civil War also witnesses the early use of land mines, first employed by the Confederacy outside Richmond in 1862. A mine is usually an artillery shell converted to explode by weight or electric current. Many on both sides despise the "dishonorable" weapon. *LOC*

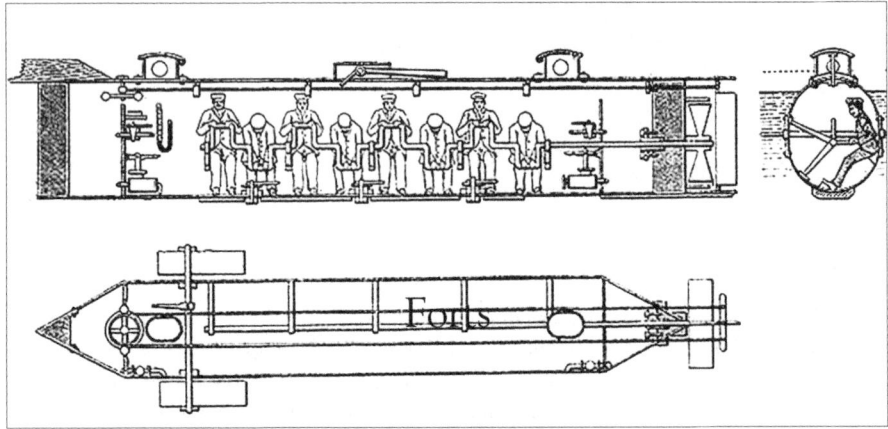

The Confederacy also pioneers underwater warfare. The *H. L. Hunley* (shown here in an early drawing by one of her designers, W. A. Alexander) is a privately commissioned 40-foot underwater "submarine" propelled by seven men turning a center crank shaft while an eighth pilots the craft. The vessel is armed with a torpedo on a spar to ram into enemy ships. It is a dangerous occupation, and the vessel sinks twice; the first drowns five men in August 1863, and the second takes the entire crew, including Hunley himself, that October. The submarine is in fact stable, as she proves after several months of successful operations. Unfortunately, on its only successful mission on February 17, 1864, it sinks the blockader USS *Housatonic* but sinks a third time with the entire crew. The *Hunley* was discovered in 1995, raised, and is now preserved at Warren Lasch Conservation Center in Charleston. *NA*

Forts

Large fortifications, especially masonry bastions erected at key locations along the American coastline to protect harbors, important cities, and approaches inland. They play a major role in the Civil War. Work began on most of them in the 1820s and 1830s, though it often took decades to complete them. Southern forces begin seizing forts and other Federal installations during the

Work on Fort Pulaski, a massive masonry fort guarding the Savannah River approach to Savannah, Georgia, began in 1827 and did not end until the late 1840s. Georgia militia seize the fort in February 1861. In early 1862, a large Union force establishes land batteries and shells the fort. The belief at this time is that large masonry forts can withstand artillery fire, but the development of rifled cannon changes that equation. The artillery rounds pierce the walls (as seen above), and Colonel Charles H. Olmstead, Pulaski's commander, surrenders. The loss of Pulaski closes Savannah harbor to the Confederates and extends Union blockading operations. LOC

An interior view of Fort Fisher near the southeast end of the mile-long bastion showing the fort's main magazine. The giant fort is built almost entirely from sand, which can withstand heavy pounding from cannons of all varieties. LOC

secession crisis. Fort Sumter, in Charleston Harbor, held out. When it was fired upon in April 1861, the shooting war began.

The various forts, from Texas up through Virginia, impacted the way both sides fought the war. Many in the South believe the masonry forts could not be taken by artillery fire alone, and even a land attack would likely prove unsuccessful. The early (and fast) fall of Fort Pulaski guarding Savannah, Georgia, quickly puts an end to that belief, and prompts the construction of massive sand batteries and forts, which are resistant to artillery attack. The largest and most effective of these is Fort Fisher outside Wilmington, North Carolina.

Fort Tyler, an earthwork fortification outside Montgomery, Alabama, is widely recognized as the last Confederate fort to surrender. It fell on April 16, 1865.

These remarkable views show Confederate Fort Johnson inside Charleston harbor, and, in the distance, Fort Sumter, which by this time has been battered by Union artillery into a pile of rubble. The forts fall into Federal hands when Charleston is evacuated in February 1865. These pictures were taken the following month. *LOC*

The evolution of Fort Sumter during the war is instructive. The interior shot (above) is taken soon after it fell to Confederate forces in April 1861. Note the extensive damage to the masonry construction, which should have been a clear warning to Confederate commanders that these types of forts are highly vulnerable to artillery fire. The Sumter interior (below) photo is taken later in the war, when gabions (usually wicker cylinders filled with sand and rock) are used to reinforce the walls. *LOC*

(Above) Inside Fort Darling (also called Drewry's Fort or simply Drewry's Bluff) at Drewry's Bluff about 80 feet above the James River south of Richmond, Virginia. The installation is located at a key bend in the river, and protects the Southern capital from Union naval forces. (Below) The sprawling and powerful earthen Confederate fort at Port Hudson, Louisiana, helps hold the Mississippi River. A major Union campaign in 1863 put it under siege, and once Vicksburg falls on July 4, Port Hudson follows five days later. This photo shows a dismounted artillery piece after the surrender. *LOC*

Caring for the Sick and Wounded

Medical care is primitive when the Civil War begins and advances are slow in coming. Antibiotics do not exist. There is no effective treatment for pneumonia, called inflammation of lungs in the 1860s. And as many soldiers soon learn, most army doctors know very little about medicine.

Troops crowd into camps; sanitation is minimal. Diseases such as diarrhea, dysentery, and typhoid fever kill tens of thousands of Confederates. Communicable diseases like measles, smallpox, and consumption (tuberculosis) kill untold thousands more.

According to the photograph, this is a field hospital for John Bell Hood's command outside Richmond, Virginia, following the battle of Seven Pines (Fair Oaks), May 31-June 1, 1862. After major battles, medical staffs on both sides convert churches, houses, and barns into field hospitals. *LOC*

The soft lead bullets cause tremendous damage because they expand when they hit tissue and, especially, bone, which breaks up into several jagged pieces the doctors cannot put back together. Many wounds to the arms and legs result in amputation. There is still no such thing as a blood transfusion, and shock kills many wounded. Doctors often pride themselves on how quickly they amputate a limb because the faster it comes off, the less blood a man loses. Wounds to the stomach often lead to death from infection. The existence of bacteria is not yet known.

Soldiers who survive wounds are shipped to hospitals to convalesce and/or sent home to recover. This creates room for the more seriously wounded or ill in overcrowded hospitals and reduces the strain on the overburdened Confederate supply system: Men on furlough have to find their own food.

(Top) A rare image of a Confederate field hospital at Cedar Mountain, where Stonewall Jackson wages a hard-fought battle with Nathaniel Banks's Union command on August 9, 1862. Note the pole used for dipping water buckets into a well. (Inset) The Roper Hospital in Charleston, South Carolina, treats civilians, Confederate soldiers, and Federal prisoners of war. Federal authorities seize the hospital in early 1865 when the city is evacuated. The hospital reopens to the public in 1867. LOC

Chimborazo hospital is a medical facility in Richmond, Virginia, used by the Confederate Army (1862-1865) and run by Dr. James B. McCaw, a professor at the Medical College of Virginia. McCaw establishes a strict organizational structure, including divisional hospitals, surgeons, assistant surgeons, acting assistant surgeons, stewards, nurses, druggists, cooks, dentists, etc. Surgeons have to have at least five years experience to work there. Nearly 80,000 patients pass through the sprawling and exceptionally well-run hospital. Its death rate is about 9%, one of the lowest of any similar hospital. *LOC*

(Above) At the outbreak of the war, Felicia Porter helps establish a hospital in Nashville, Tennessee, and later serves as president of the Women's Relief Society, a group that raises money for sick and wounded soldiers. After the war the society raises funds for artificial legs for ex-Confederates. *Photographic History of the Civil War*

At the outset of the war, the Confederacy is reluctant to use women as volunteer nurses, much less pay them. Kate Cumming (above) volunteers at a hospital at Corinth, Mississippi, to tend wounded from Shiloh. As a paid nurse she works in a Chattanooga, Tennessee, hospital. After Chattanooga falls, Cumming serves in a number of hospitals in Georgia. Her 1866 book, *A Journal of Hospital Life in the Confederate Army of Tennessee from the Battle of Shiloh to the End of the War*, chronicles her service as a nurse.

A Journal of Hospital Life in the Confederate Army of Tennessee from the Battle of Shiloh to the End of the War

(Above) Confederate wounded at Smith's barn, with Dr. Anson Hurd of the 14th Indiana in attendance. When no buildings are readily available, medical staff erect tents. This small field hospital is located near Keedysville, Maryland, to treat wounded and captured Confederates immediately after the battle of Sharpsburg. (Below) Wounded Confederate and Union soldiers are often treated together. Here, Southern prisoners and wounded Union soldiers await medical care after the battle of Spotsylvania Court House (May 8-21, 1864) in Virginia. *Photographic History of the Civil War*

Prisoners of War

In the first year of the war, the Confederacy and the Union have no formal agreement for exchanging prisoners. After the Seven Days' battles, Major Generals D. H. Hill (CSA) and John A. Dix (USA) hammer out an agreement formalizing prisoner exchanges. Under the Dix-Hill Cartel, men are exchanged as quickly as possible.

By mid-1863, large-scale exchanges have largely ceased. Union leaders don't want to swap a Confederate, who fights for the duration of the war, for a Union soldier whose enlistment might soon expire. Union officials also complain that Confederates refuse to exchange or parole African-American

Washington's Old Capitol Prison holds both captured Confederate soldiers and political prisoners. Today, the United States Supreme Court building occupies the site. *LOC*

The *New York* carrying exchanged POWs. The exchange system crafted in the Dix-Hill Cartel works reasonably well for about a year: One private for one private, one sergeant for one sergeant, etc. Only after a proper exchange can both prisoners return to their units and fight. After 10 days, however, whoever is not exchanged has to be paroled and promise not to serve in a military capacity unless formally exchanged. LOC

prisoners since many are former slaves. The exchange system breaks down. Both sides build new prisons. By mid-1864, Confederate POWs are housed in prisons ranging from Point Lookout, Maryland, to Jefferson Barracks outside St. Louis, Missouri.

Both sides segregate officers from enlisted men, partly to prevent officers from originating attempts to break out of prison. Most Southern officers are shipped to Johnson's Island in Lake Erie's Sandusky Bay. Northern POWs are held in Richmond's Libby Prison or on Belle Isle, also in Richmond. Death tolls rise with prisoners crammed into hastily built camps.

After the war, the US Quartermaster General establishes National Cemeteries to protect the graves of the 25,961 Union men who die in Southern prisons. In 1912, the commissioner tasked with marking Confederate graves in the North reports 25,560 burials, which does not include hundreds who died in Union custody in the South and are buried in cemeteries from Hampton, Virginia, to Ship Island, Mississippi. An estimated 27,000 Confederates die while Federal prisoners.

(Above) A rarely seen photograph of Confederate soldiers captured in fighting at Aldie, Virginia, on June 17, 1863, during the early weeks of the Gettysburg Campaign. The exchange arrangement begins breaking down in 1863 when the Union stops exchanging prisoners in violation of the Dix-Hill Cartel. By August 1863, the prisoner system breaks down completely and large-scale exchanges cease. The establishment of prison camps, filled with growing numbers of prisoners, begins in earnest.

(Below) Confederate prisoners captured on April 1, 1865, at the Battle of Five Forks in Virginia. These men don't know the war is nearly at an end—a very fortunate circumstance for them. *LOC*

(Above) Confederate prisoners captured in the spring of 1862 during the Shenandoah Valley Campaign, guarded in a Union camp. LOC

(Below) Prison camps are located near railroads to facilitate the shipment of prisoners. These captured Confederates wait at the depot in Chattanooga, Tennessee. LOC

(Above) Prisoners answer roll call twice a day to discourage escape attempts from Elmira Prison in New York. Some 2,298 Confederates and 24 civilians (most of whom were political prisoners) die at Elmira. Hundreds of thousands are taken prisoner during the war. In 1912, the commissioner tasked with marking the graves of Confederate soldiers, sailors, and civilians (political prisoners) in the North reports marking 25,560 graves. This does not include the hundreds of Confederates who die in Union custody in the South. Men are buried in cemeteries from Hampton, Virginia, to Ship Island, Mississippi. An estimated 27,000 Confederates die while Federal prisoners. By 1868, the Union Quartermaster General reports that 25,971 Union soldiers died in Confederate prisons. Some 12,461 Federal soldiers died at Camp Sumter Military Prison at Andersonville, Georgia. LOC

During February 1863, nearly one of every ten Confederates held in the Union prison at Chicago's Camp Douglas (right) die. During the war, 4,457 Confederates die at Camp Douglas. LOC

(Below) Union prison camp commanders use different forms of punishment to control prisoners. These captives at Rock Island, Illinois, are "riding Mulligan's mule," an uncomfortable and ultimately painful penalty for breaking some rule. *Stereoview image courtesy Rock Island Arsenal Museum*

(Bottom) After the war ended, Southern POWs are required to take the Oath of Allegiance to the United States before they can be released. The prisoners in this photo are taking the oath at Rock Island, Illinois. *Stereoview image courtesy Rock Island Arsenal Museum*

One of the iconic images from the Civil War: Three Confederate soldiers as they appeared in the field, captured at Gettysburg. According to photographic historian William A. Frassanito, this photo is likely taken on July 15, 1863, the day before some 2,500 Confederate prisoners are sent to various prison camps in the North. *LOC*

The War on the Water

President Jefferson Davis appoints Stephen Mallory as Secretary of the Navy. The former chairman of the Naval Affairs Committee for the United States Senate is the perfect man for the job, and the only man in the cabinet who will hold his original position throughout the war. His mission is exceedingly difficult because there is no Southern navy when the Civil War breaks out.

Mallory knows the South cannot compete with the much larger Union navy and its seven decades of tradition and experience, so he decides on three objectives: Make the war as expensive as possible by attacking Union merchant shipping worldwide; protect Southern harbors, rivers, and the seacoast from invasion; and use mostly private vessels to run the Northern blockade to siphon off Union ship assets.

A large part of Mallory's plan involves the construction of ironclad ships of war and development of better naval artillery. The Confederacy's only real navy yard for building and repairing ocean-going ships, however, is at Pensacola, Florida. When the Union evacuates the Gosport Yard at Portsmouth, Virginia, Mallory takes it over, refloats the burned steamer USS *Merrimack*, and converts her into the ironclad CSS *Virginia*. The mammoth iron ship steamed into Hampton Roads on March 8, 1862, and sank two large wooden warships, but met the new Northern ironclad USS *Monitor* the next day. The famous "Battle of the Ironclads" was essentially a draw, but it is the dawn of a new era.

Mallory's ironclad navy effectively blocked and protected several important harbors for most of the war, and helped hold inland rivers. Southern commerce raiders, like the CSS *Alabama* and CSS *Shenandoah*, successfully roamed the world's oceans and sank dozens of ships. The submarine *Hunley* sank the first warship in history in early 1864 outside Charleston harbor, and underwater torpedoes (mines) wreaked havoc on Union assets, including the warship USS *Cairo*, which sank in the Yazoo River.

Secretary of the Navy Stephen M. Mallory (1812-1873). The native Floridian and US Senator is not keen on secession, but joins the Confederacy when Florida leaves the Union. Mallory is not a sailor, but he learns a significant amount about naval matters serving as chairman of the Senate Committee on Naval Affairs. His knowledge helps shape the new navy and its objectives. Some of his ideas, such as building iron ships, are successful and adopted by other countries. He is held prisoner after the war and released without charges. Mallory dies in Pensacola of heart failure. *LOC*

(Above) The CSS (Confederate States Ship) *Teaser* is a civilian tugboat converted into a gunboat. The *Teaser* patrols the James River during the war's early months until the USS *Maratanza* captures her on July 4, 1862. The Union navy christens her USS *Teaser* and she steams the waters of the Potomac River from Alexandria, Virginia, south to Point Lookout, Maryland, to interdict Southern blockade runners. (Below) A Federal sailor stands beside the captured CSS *Teaser*'s large cannon which fires a shell weighing 100 pounds. *LOC*

(Above) The former Civil War blockade-runner *Chicora* in a postwar view on the Great Lakes in 1868. A number of other small craft, the largest of which has two masts, can be seen off her stern. The Liverpool-built steamer is built earlier in 1864 and commissioned by the Chicora Import & Export Company. (Bottom) The "Cottonclad" side-wheel steamer CSS *General Bragg*. Cotton is much more plentiful than iron in the Confederacy, so Confederate naval officials use cotton in place of iron to protect the ships. The CSS *General Bragg* operates on the Mississippi River until she is captured at Memphis in 1862. *LOC*

(Above) The CSS *Robert E. Lee* runs the Union blockade more than twenty times before she is captured near Wilmington, North Carolina, in November 1863. Outfitted as a warship, she helps enforce the Union naval blockade as the USS *Fort Donelson*. LOC

(Bottom) The British-built blockade runner *Ruby* slips past the Federal blockaders at Charleston, South Carolina, only to run aground on Folly Island in June 1863. LOC

Franklin Buchanan (1800-1874) is the only full admiral in the Confederate Navy (1862). He commands the ironclad CSS *Virginia* on March 8, 1862, but is wounded in the leg and, to his lasting regret, unable to lead his ship the next day in the famous battle with the USS *Monitor* (an honor that goes to his executive officer, Catesby Jones). Buchanan is sent to Mobile, Alabama, where he commands the ironclad CSS *Tennessee* in the Battle of Mobile Bay on August 5, 1864, and is wounded and captured. LOC

Matthew Fontaine Maury (1806-1873) is a former US naval officer and a man of science. He joins the new Confederacy as its Chief of Sea Coast, River, and Harbor Defenses. He spends much of the war abroad seeking support for the South's navy. Maury, who understands the flow of electricity through wires underwater, perfects an "electric torpedo" (naval mine), which according to a Federal report, sinks "more vessels than all other causes combined." LOC

Confederate agents order an ironclad warship from a French shipyard in 1864. The French government attempts to block the sale of the ship. The ironclad is commissioned as the *CSS Stonewall* in January 1865, but arrives too late to aid the Confederate cause. *LOC*

The Home Front

The Southern home front feels the brunt of war almost immediately. Tens of thousands of men leave their homes for front, placing an immediate burden on the women and children left behind.

The role of women changes. Women are now heads of the households, work in military hospitals, as teachers, and even as government clerks. Wives of plantation owners often become managers of the plantation—a task few are prepared to perform. The wives of small farmers work in the fields, care for the animals, and tend to their children.

Travelers and furloughed soldiers are some of the best sources of news about the war. These civilians are waiting at Hanover Junction, Virginia, for news from the front.

Photographic History of the Civil War

As Confederate officials transport wounded and sick away from the front lines hospitals spring up in cities and towns along railroad tracks. Southern women with no training are pressed into service as nurses. When one volunteer nurse is asked why she nurses strangers she replies, "My sons are in the Confederate Army. If my sons need nursing I hope someone will help them."

Many women also migrate to cities and work long hours in cotton mills and other manufacturing plants. Some perform dangerous work in laboratories assembling musket cartridges, primers, and explosive shells. In March 1863, for example, an explosion rocks the Confederate laboratory on Brown's Island near Richmond killing at least 45, many of whom are women. The unlucky ones linger for days before succumbing to their burns.

The war brings about many shortages, including clothing. The army needs wool for uniforms and blankets, but little is grown in the Southern states. Most has to be imported through the increasingly effective Union naval blockade, leaving little for those back home.

Money was another problem. The Confederacy had little choice but to print paper money to fund the war, which immediately brings about inflation and increasing prices for everyday items. Eight months into the war, inflation was about 12% per month. Household staples like corn meal, wheat, flour, meat, and even salt became too expensive for the ordinary family. Food riots break out in Mobile, Atlanta, Richmond, and elsewhere.

Late in the war Southern civilians suffer when the war reaches their home-front. Sherman's armies burn their way from Atlanta to the sea and then

into the Carolinas. While Sherman's March to the Sea is more infamous, Philip Sheridan's men slaughter livestock and burn crops, barns, and grain mills during the Shenandoah Valley Campaign—a harsh tactic he would later also use against the Plains Indians.

This unidentified woman wears a mourning brooch and displays a framed image of an unidentified soldier. *LOC*

Although customs vary, most women who lose husbands during the war wear some type of mourning clothing after their death. The unidentified young girl in the photograph above is wearing a mourning brooch and holds a photograph of a soldier. Given her obvious young age, it is most likely her deceased father. She is also wearing mourning ribbons and a mourning dress. *LOC*

An unknown number of women serve as guides and spies for the Confederacy. Nancy Hart (top) begins aiding the Southern cause after Union soldiers murder her civilian brother-in-law. While Nancy Hart actually rides with a band of partisan rangers, Belle Boyd (bottom) concentrates her efforts on spying. She is imprisoned three times during the war. In March of 1864, she attempts to reach England, but her ship is intercepted by a Union blockader and she is sent to Canada, where she meets a Union naval officer. She eventually marries him—in England. *Photographic History of the War*

Rhoda Ray (right) and her children live on her master's farm in southwestern Missouri. During the Battle of Oak Hills (Wilson's Creek) Ray, who is in her 30s, seeks refuge in the cellar of her master's (John Ray's) farmhouse. When the house is converted into a makeshift hospital, Ray nurses wounded Confederates there. Because southwestern Missouri is not in "rebellion" on January 1, 1863, when the Emancipation Proclamation goes into effect, she is not freed until 1865. This photo is taken after the war. She dies in 1897. *WICR 01755MM in the collection of Wilson's Creek National Battlefield. Image courtesy of the National Park Service*

Dr. Reuben Samuel (left) marries Zerelda James, mother of Frank and Jesse James, in 1855. During the war Federal militia searches for Frank James, a member of Quantrill's Confederate guerrillas, and tries to force Dr. Samuel to reveal Frank's whereabouts by hanging him. The doctor survives, but suffers permanent brain damage. *WICR 30207 in the collection of Wilson's Creek National Battlefield. Image courtesy of the National Park Service*

Atlanta, Georgia, a view along Whitehall Street in 1864. The South is overwhelmingly rural. In 1860, only 9,554 people live in Atlanta. As the war progresses, people flock to Atlanta to work in factories supplying materials for the Confederacy. This photograph, which shows the width of Whitehall Street and the diversity of architecture, is taken shortly before the burning of Atlanta in November of 1864. *LOC*

Although Baton Rouge, Louisiana, began the war deep inside the Confederacy, war arrives quickly. By 1861 Baton Rouge is a thriving Mississippi River town and home to more than 5,000. The war collapses its economy, and the only businesses that thrive are those supplying Union forces that occupy the city in the spring of 1862. That summer, a small command of Confederate troops under General John C. Breckinridge try unsuccessfully to recapture the city. The houses in this photo are destroyed on the order of Union Colonel Halbert E. Paine to give his soldiers a better field of fire. *Photographic History of the Civil War*

(Above) The lovely Marye house on Marye's Heights above Fredericksburg, Virginia, escapes complete destruction, but is heavily damaged during Federal occupation. Soldiers also dig rifle pits on the sprawling lawn. (Bottom) The destroyed homes in Fredericksburg are demolished during a massive Union artillery bombardment on December 11, 1862, to drive Confederate infantry of General Lee's Army of Northern Virginia away so the bulk of the Army of the Potomac could cross. *LOC*

The War Ends

The Civil War came to an end in spasms, one army surrendering after another, rather than all at one time. By mid-March of 1865, Confederate forces are in dire straits. Union General U. S. Grant's forces have General Lee's Confederates—the largest and most important field army—pinned in the trenches defending Petersburg and Richmond. General Sherman's Federals are marching through North Carolina, where an attack on March 19 by General Joseph Johnston's Confederates at Bentonville proves unable to stop Northern progress.

Lee's lines became impossible to hold when his far right at Five Forks is crushed on April 1 exposing the Southside Railroad to destruction. Grant orders an attack along the entire front before dawn on the morning of April 2, and the Southern front collapses.

Fort Mahone (Damnation), a strong position south of Petersburg, falls on the morning of April 2, 1865. This unlucky Confederate dies in the muddy trenches defending it. LOC

After Richmond falls, photographers record the scenes of devastation including the smokestack from the ironclad CSS *Virginia II*. The warship is hit repeatedly when it, together with ironclads CSS *Fredericksburg* and *Richmond*, raid down the James River the previous February. All three rams are destroyed during the city's evacuation. LOC

Lee evacuates Richmond and Petersburg, and marches west as fast as possible ahead of Union pursuit so he can turn south to join up with General Johnston in North Carolina. Grant pushes troops quickly west in pursuit fighting several engagements and running skirmishes. Union forces cut off and capture some 7,000 of Lee's men at Sayler's Creek on April 6. Lee surrenders the Army of Northern Virginia at Appomattox Court House on April 9, 1865. Johnston surrenders in North Carolina on April 26 to Sherman.

Other commands cease fighting and surrender across what is left of the Confederacy. Cherokee Stand Watie, a Southern general, does not surrender until June 23 at Fort Towson, in the Chocktaw Nations area in what is today southeastern Oklahoma. The final surrender was the raider CSS *Shenandoah* on November 6, 1865, in Liverpool, England.

A drawing of the surrender of Confederates at Sayler's (Sailor's) Creek on April 6, 1865, one of the battles waged during General Lee's retreat west out of Richmond and Petersburg. Lee watches from afar as men surrender *en masse* and declares, "My God, has the army dissolved?" Southern losses at Sayler's Creek—7,700, about one-fifth of Lee's army—include at least nine generals. *LOC*

When he discovered that his route south was blocked by Grant's Union forces, Lee surrendered his army on April 9, 1865, at Appomattox in the Wilmer McLean house, which is pictured here. *LOC*

The James Bennett Farm, in Durham, North Carolina, where Gen. Joseph E. Johnston surrenders his army (comprised of a motley collection of commands) to Maj. Gen. William T. Sherman 17 days after General Lee at Appomattox on April 26, 1865. Johnston's capitulation ends the war in the Carolinas, Georgia, and Florida. LOC

Date	Confederate Commander	Number of Troops Surrendered	Troops Surrendered/Location
April 9, 1865	Robert E. Lee	26,765	Army of Northern Virginia
April 26, 1865	Joseph Johnston	29,924	Carolinas
May 4, 1865	Richard Taylor	10,000	east of the Mississippi
May 26, 1865	Kirby Smith	20,000	Trans-Mississippi (west of the Mississippi)

Remembering the War, Healing the Wounds

Once the war was over, the hundreds of thousands of Southern men returned home. Most walked, sometimes hundreds of miles, often not knowing what they would find once they got there. The war ravaged the Southern states. Reuniting families, finding work, and rebuilding their lives were the top priorities.

Confederate veterans gather regularly with former comrades to recall their wartime experiences. These elderly former Confederates, pictured here in 1917, fought with General Nathan B. Forrest's cavalry. *LOC*

After the war, Southern women form the Ladies' Memorial societies to properly mark and care for the remains of Confederate dead. In 1890, the Ladies' Memorial Association of Petersburg (Virginia) erected this arch to memorialize the 20,000 Confederates buried in that city's Blandford Cemetery. Nearly 17,000 are unknown. *Author*

Everything had changed. The scale of death and the large number of wounded who survived create unprecedented physical and emotional challenges. Some four million slaves are now free, their future and that of their former owners yet unknown.

Former slave owners have land to cultivate, but little or no money to pay for labor. Former slaves and white laborers need work. A system called "sharecropping," where the landowner supplies seed, tools, housing, and perhaps a mule to a sharecropper who works part of the large farm, takes root. The landowner often arranges credit for men sharecropping his land. After the crop is harvested, the landowner and the sharecropper share the profits.

The sharecropping system is abused by dishonest landowners, but the system worked much better than the promise of "40 acres and a mule" made by Northern Carpetbaggers. The need for workers in defense plants during World War II reduces sharecropping, but a form of it still exists: Many poultry farmers still contract with large corporations to raise chickens and turkeys.

Beginning in the 1870s, former Confederates began to argue that the South fought a heroic war and was not beaten, but lost because of superior numbers and resources. The "Lost Cause," as it came to be known, grew to become a strong cultural force. It became important to locate and mark graves. Southern

(Above) In 1913, the 50th anniversary of Gettysburg (July 1-3, 1863), more than 45,000 Union and 8,000 Confederate veterans poured into Gettysburg for a massive joint reunion. The Confederates shown here are recreating Pickett's Charge. (Below) "Glad to meet you." As young men, these veterans fought one another at Gettysburg. Their 1913 encounter, pictured here at the battlefield's famous "Angle," proved more cordial. *LOC*

women in Ladies Memorial Associations raised funds, erected monuments, and helped re-inter Confederate dead.

In time, a national consensus developed that enabled the former warring sections to reconcile around the mutual valor and sacrifice of their soldiers.

For years, Federal Law prevents the graves of Confederates buried in national cemeteries from being marked. This changes in 1906, when Congress authorizes headstones for Confederate prisoners buried in Arlington National Cemetery. In this image, crowds gather to hear President Woodrow Wilson speak at the unveiling of Arlington's Confederate Monument on June 4, 1914. *LOC*

Peace at last: Two former enemies shake hands at the 1913 Gettysburg reunion. *Fiftieth Anniversary of the Battle of Gettysburg*

Gallery of Confederate Soldiers

These soldiers were not all heroes. At least one was a thief and several went AWOL. Their ages, social standing, and backgrounds varied, but they had one thing in common: They all wore the butternut and gray.

Private Parris P. Casey, Company I (Cherokee Rangers), 19th Alabama Infantry in August 1861. He dies in a hospital in November 1862 at Clearfield, Tennessee. In 1864, his father files a death compensation claim with the Confederate Government. *LOC*

John Wyeth (left) is too young to join the Confederate Army in 1862, so he rides with Gen. John Hunt Morgan as an "independent scout." He later joins the 4th Alabama Cavalry and fights under Gen. Forrest's command. Private Wyeth fights in a number of skirmishes before he sees real combat at Chickamauga. He is captured in the Sequatchie Valley after raiding a Federal wagon train carrying supplies to Chattanooga. Wyeth spends most of his 16 months as a prisoner at Camp Morton near Indianapolis. Wyeth attends medical school after the war. Convinced the lecture-only method of medical training needs revision, in 1881 he begins the New York Polyclinic Graduate Medical School and Hospital in 1881. William and Charles Mayo, who later found the Mayo Clinic, are members of the first class. Wyeth serves as President of the American Medical Association in 1906 and 1908 and writes several articles and medical books, including *That Devil Forrest: Life of General Nathan Bedford Forrest*. His autobiography, *With Sabre and Scalpel: The Autobiography of a Soldier and Surgeon*, is deceiving. Wyeth never carried a sabre in combat.

John L. Carter (right) is 21 years old when he enlists in the Autauga Rifles (Company G), 6th Alabama Infantry in March 1862. He is soon detailed as a wagon-master (teamster) and is paid a bonus of 25 cents a day. He is captured near Gettysburg, Pennsylvania, on July 4, 1863, but released. He returns to his regiment, where he resumes driving the regimental "public wagon." After the war, Carter returns to Autauga County, Alabama, lives a long life, and dies in 1907. *Joseph W. Willis*

Thomas **Bolding's** (right) military career is brief. He enlists in Company G, 24th Arkansas Infantry on June 19, 1862, and in December is listed as absent without leave (AWOL). *WICR 3022 in the collection of Wilson's Creek National Battlefield. Image courtesy of National Park Service*

James McDavid Flynt (left) enlists in Company D, 2nd Arkansas Infantry in June 1862, fights at Perryville in Kentucky, dies at Murfreesboro (Stone's River), Tennessee, and is put into an unmarked grave. *WICR 31556 in the collection of Wilson's Creek National Battlefield. Image courtesy of the National Park Service*

Jacob Whetstone (right) enlists in the 4th Arkansas Infantry on November 22, 1861. He likely fights at the Battle of Elkhorn Tavern (Pea Ridge) in March 1862. He is mortally wounded on June 1, 1862, and dies three days later. Neither the name of the fight or the site of his burial are recorded. *Pea Ridge National Military Park*

Records on **William P. Ward's** military service are scarce. Ward enlists in the 41st Georgia Infantry in March 1862. The 41st sees combat at Perryville, Kentucky, before serving in the defense of Vicksburg, Mississippi, where Ward is captured. After he is exchanged, he returns to his regiment, which fights in the battles around Chattanooga. Ward likely fights at Franklin and Nashville, Tennessee, and at Bentonville, North Carolina. When he surrenders at Bennett Place in late April 1865, however, his name is on the surrender documents as a member of the 40th Georgia. *LOC*

Philip Cook (right) enters Confederate service as a private in 1861 in the 4th Georgia Infantry. He is soon appointed as an adjutant and serves as a staff officer. His outstanding field service elevates him to colonel in November 1862, wounded at Chancellorsville, and misses Gettysburg. Promoted to general in the summer of 1864, he is wounded and captured leading his brigade against Fort Stedman on March 25, 1865. Cook is elected to Congress in 1873, and dies in 1894. *LOC*

Without modern antibiotics many soldiers fall victim to disease. One is **Sampson Altman, Jr.** (left), who enlists in Company C, 29th Georgia Volunteers, at Savannah on October 4, 1861. Altman dies of pneumonia on April 27, 1862, in Augusta, Georgia. *LOC*

John H. King (right) of the 40th Georgia Infantry receives his "baptism of fire" in a skirmish at Tazewell, Virginia. He is captured at Vicksburg, exchanged, and rejoins his regiment. In January 1864 he is shot in the neck and captured in a skirmish near Sevierville, Tennessee. A Union surgeon declares King's wound mortal, but he survives and is imprisoned at Camp Chase, Ohio. In 1904, King, now surgeon of the Confederate Soldiers Home in Atlanta, writes about his experiences as a POW in *Three Hundred Days in a Yankee Prison*. *LOC*

The LaRoque Family

John G. LaRoque (left) is an overseer on a large Georgia plantation before he enlists in Company E, 4th Georgia Infantry. His wife **Nancy ("Nannie") LaRoque** (below) is pregnant and their son **John W. "Little Willie"** (bottom) is born less than four weeks later on June 26, 1861. *Ralph Mills*

John does not see his son until November 1861, when he gets a 20-day furlough. "Little Willie" dies on August 3, 1862, just 13 months old, while John is fighting with Robert E. Lee's Army of Northern Virginia. *Ralph Mills*

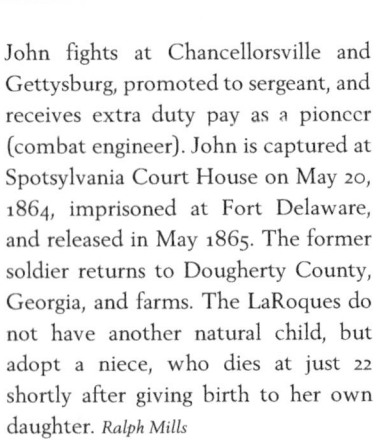

John fights at Chancellorsville and Gettysburg, promoted to sergeant, and receives extra duty pay as a pioneer (combat engineer). John is captured at Spotsylvania Court House on May 20, 1864, imprisoned at Fort Delaware, and released in May 1865. The former soldier returns to Dougherty County, Georgia, and farms. The LaRoques do not have another natural child, but adopt a niece, who dies at just 22 shortly after giving birth to her own daughter. *Ralph Mills*

Kentucky officially remains in the Union, but many Kentuckians join Southern units. **Thomas McCreary** (also spelled McCrary), seen here in a Columbus depot jacket holding what may be a Bible, serves in Company E, 3rd Kentucky Cavalry. He is a member of Maj. Gen. John Hunt Morgan's command when he is captured at Lebanon, Kentucky, on July 5, 1863. McCreary is sent to Louisville Military Prison before being shipped to Camp Morton in Indianapolis. Three weeks later he is transferred to Camp Douglas in Chicago, and there his trail ends. Nothing more about him is known. *LOC*

Confederate records can be difficult to decipher. **Albert Estopinal** (left) was barely 17 when he enlists as an orderly sergeant in a Louisiana Infantry regiment. Records at the National Archives show he enlisted in both the 22nd and 28th Louisiana infantry regiments on the same day. Estopinal was detailed as a commissary sergeant during the Vicksburg Campaign. Both regimental Compiled Service Records claim he surrenders at Meridian, Mississippi, in 1865. After the war he is active in politics as St. Bernard Parish assessor, sheriff, state representative, state senator, and lieutenant governor of Louisiana. He ends his political career as an US congressman (1908-1919). *LOC*

James W. Nicholson (right) teaches school before he enlists in the 12th Louisiana Infantry. He fights in many of the battles in the Western Theater, including Baker's Creek (Champion Hill) and Jackson, both in Mississippi. Sergeant Nicholson is detailed as a commissary sergeant in August 1863 and the following May as a nurse. He fights at Bentonville in North Carolina in March of 1865 and surrenders in that state with the 12th Louisiana Infantry. Nicholson walks home to Louisiana, a trip that takes him 35 days. After the war he serves two terms as the president of Louisiana State University. *LOC*

Twenty-four-year-old **Albert B. Martin** (seen above sporting an Edmond's hat) works as a clerk in civilian life before enlisting in the 3rd Company of the famous Washington Louisiana Light Artillery on May 2, 1861. On December 24, 1861, he was sentenced to serve seven years in the Richmond Virginia Penitentiary for "robbing the mail." *LOC*

John P. Renwick (left) enlists as a private in the 3rd Louisiana Infantry in May 1861. He rises through the ranks to become the unit's sergeant major. Less than four months after his enlistment, he is killed in his first battle at Oak Hills (Wilson's Creek) in Missouri. *WICR 30835 in the collection of Wilson's Creek National Battlefield. Image courtesy of the National Park Service*

John L. Rapier (right), 19, enlists in Co. A, 7th Battalion, Louisiana Infantry, at New Orleans on April 22, 1861. He is wounded on July 11, 1862, "around Richmond." He survives and that October is promoted to sergeant major. He transfers to the Confederate States Zouave Battalion of Louisiana Volunteers and in April 1863 is commissioned as an officer in the Confederate Marine Corps. *LOC*

Most Confederate enlisted men are farmers, but **David J. Hill** (right), 33, is a surveyor. He enlists in the 2nd Mississippi in March 1861, fights at First Manassas (Bull Run), and is detailed as "Baggage [supply train] Guard" for much of 1862. He is wounded in the leg and captured during Pickett's Charge at Gettysburg, exchanged, and hospitalized. After a 30-day furlough, he returns to his unit in the fall of 1863 and detailed as the brigade's shoemaker. Hill is captured at Hatcher's Run on April 3, 1865, and soon thereafter returns home to Mississippi. *Sonny Hill*

Private William "Billy" Blake (right) of the 18th Mississippi, part of William Barksdale's famous brigade, is shot in the leg at Gettysburg on July 2, 1863. He lies helplessly on the field for more than 24 hours before being carried to a field hospital, where a Federal surgeon amputates one of his legs near the hip. Blake defies the odds and survives his wound and his medical care, and resigns from the Confederate Army after being fitted with a wooden leg in November 1864. After the war he moves to New Orleans, Louisiana, and raises a large family. *Dinkins, An Old Johnnie*

Mississippi native James Dinkins (left) is just 14 when his father enrolls him in military school at Charlotte, North Carolina. When the war breaks out Dinkins bribes a telegraph operator to write a fake telegram so he can join the 1st North Carolina Infantry (a six-month unit). Dinkins undergoes his baptism of fire at Big Bethel, Virginia, on June 10, 1861. After his enlistment expires, he returns to Mississippi and joins the 18th Mississippi, which moves back to Virginia. Dinkins's body servant (slave) accompanies him. He fights in many battles, including the Seven Days' Battles, Second Manassas, Sharpsburg (Antietam), and the combat at Fredericksburg. In the spring of 1863 Dinkins is promoted to lieutenant and spends most of the rest of the war serving in General Nathan Bedford Forrest's Cavalry. *Dinkins, An Old Johnnie*

Private Silas A. Shirley of the 16th Mississippi Infantry poses for his photograph with a sign reading "Victory or Death!" He serves through much of the war with his regiment in Carnot Posey's brigade until that officer is killed at Bristoe Station in October 1863. Colonel Nathaniel Harris of the 19th Mississippi assumes command of the brigade and capably leads it through the Wilderness and during the long bloody action at Spotsylvania Court House. Harris is called upon to help stem the massive breakthrough in the middle of Lee's lines on May 12, 1864. Shirley is killed in the bloody action. *LOC*

Henry Augustus Moore (right) enlists in Company F of the 15th Mississippi Infantry on May 8, 1862, just a month after Shiloh. He poses with a sign reading, "Jeff Davis and the South!" Moore dies that summer in north-central Mississippi at Water Valley, (Yalobusha County) on August 15. The cause of death is not recorded. *LOC*

Joseph B. Wright, age 23 (right), is a minister in Randolph County, Missouri, when he enlists in Company G, 5th Missouri Infantry. He fights in several battles including Elk Horn Tavern (Pea Ridge) before being commissioned chaplain for the 1st Missouri Cavalry in 1863. *WICR 11462 in the collection of Wilson's Creek National Battlefield. Image courtesy of the National Park Service*

(Left) A native of Lincoln County, North Carolina, 21-year old farmer **Reuben Goodson** enlists in the 52nd North Carolina Infantry while the regiment is organizing in April 1862. He dies of acute dysentery in a hospital in Richmond, Virginia, on June 6, 1864. *LOC*

George E. Gibbs (left) is a carpenter before he enlists in the Missouri State Guard. He musters out after six months of service and joins an artillery unit stationed at Columbus, Kentucky. While serving on Island Number 10 on the Mississippi River, Union troops under Maj. Gen. John Pope force the Confederates to surrender. Gibbs is sent to Camp Douglas in Chicago, and is paroled in 1863. He works as a carpenter in Illinois until he returns to Missouri in 1869. *WICR 11458 in the collection of Wilson's Creek National Battlefield. Image courtesy of the National Park Service*

David Henderson Duvall is one of three Missouri brothers (see facing page for more information). *WICR 30172 in the collection of Wilson's Creek National Battlefield. Image courtesy of the National Park Service*

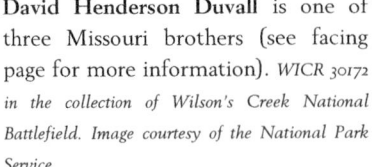

The three Duvall brothers—**William** (25, right), **Thomas** (21, left), and **David Henderson** (19, opposite page)—are farmers before the war. They fight with the Missouri State Guard at Oak Hills (Wilson's Creek) and Lexington, Missouri, then enlist in Company C, 3rd Missouri Infantry later in 1861. The trio fight together at Elkhorn Tavern (Pea Ridge) in Arkansas, and William is promoted "from the ranks" to 2nd Lieutenant in May 1862. David Henderson spends most of July and August of 1862 in the hospital. The three brothers reunite and fight at the Battle of Iuka in Mississippi on September 19, 1862. The next month, 2nd Lieutenant William Duvall dies leading a charge during Maj. Gen. Sterling Price's failed attempt to retake Corinth, Mississippi, on October 4. Thomas and Henderson are both killed in the Battle of Baker's Creek (Champion Hill), Mississippi on May 16, 1863. Thomas is reported "mortally wounded and left on the field." All three are buried in unmarked graves. *WICR 30171 in the collection of Wilson's Creek National Battlefield. Image courtesy of the National Park Service*

While many Confederate veterans write books about their wartime experiences, **Louis Leon** (left) takes a different approach and publishes his journal entitled *Diary of a Tar Heel Confederate Soldier*. The diary records his six months in the 1st North Carolina Infantry Regiment and the balance of his service in the 53rd North Carolina Infantry. Leon fights at the early-war battle of Big Bethel in Virginia and in July 1863 at Gettysburg, Pennsylvania. Detailed as a sharpshooter, he is captured near the Wilderness in May 1864 and shipped to Point Lookout Prison and thereafter the infamous Elmira Prison. *Diary of a Tar Heel Confederate Soldier*

Private W. T. Harbison served in Company B of the 11th North Carolina Infantry. June turns out to be Harbison's unlucky month. He spends part of June 1863 in a hospital in Charlottesville, Virginia, recovering from an illness. The next June he is wounded and is sent to a Richmond hospital, where doctors amputate his lower right leg. When Harbison fails to return from a 60-day furlough, he is officially declared Absent Without Leave (AWOL). *LOC*

During the Seven Days' Battles in late June and early July 1862, Gen. Robert E. Lee's Confederate army loses 3,478 men killed in action. One of these is 21-year-old **Private William H. Rockwell** (right) of the 18th North Carolina Infantry, part of Brig. Gen. Lawrence O'Bryan Branch's brigade. Rockwell was a native of Columbus County, North Carolina. *LOC*

An unidentified soldier (left) with North Carolina state seal buttons and Company F, 3rd North Carolina Volunteers (13th North Carolina Infantry) cap stares into the camera in what is likely the first, and perhaps only, photograph he ever sits for. *LOC*

Lewis Hicks (right) enlists in Company H, 53rd North Carolina Infantry, on May 2, 1863. His company's muster roll for February 1864 notes: "Supposed to be dead but no official report [of] when or where can be found." In fact, Hicks died on July 20, 1863, at Winchester, Virginia. The Confederate Cemetery records at Winchester do not list a cause of death. *LOC*

Andrew Jackson Hughes (left) enlists in the Cleveland Guards (Company E), 12th North Carolina Infantry one week after the war erupts. He is captured at the Battle of Hanover Court House on May 27, 1862, and shipped to Fort Columbus in New York City's harbor. Once exchanged, he fights at the battles of Fredericksburg, Chancellorsville, and the Wilderness. His luck runs out at Spotsylvania Court House, where he is wounded, but refuses to allow a Confederate surgeon to amputate his arm because "that was what killed Stonewall Jackson." Hughes survives. After the war he farms in Cleveland County. His son won the Pulitzer Prize for drama, and his great-great-grandson is the author of this book. *Author*

John Stikeleather (right) is "too young to vote" when he enlists in the 4th North Carolina Infantry. A native of Iredell County, North Carolina, Stikeleather is appointed as the regimental color bearer shortly before the Seven Days' Battles, and appointed ensign in April 1864. His service as colorbearer is interrupted by three stints in hospitals. Stikeleather survives being shot in the face at the Battle of Cedar Creek in 1864. He rejoins his unit in the Petersburg trenches and surrenders at Appomattox Court House in April 1865. After the war Stikeleather serves as a North Carolina Highway Commissioner. *Graham Smith*

Private James Dodd (right) is a member of the Company C, 4th South Carolina Cavalry. He serves most of his time in the Department of South Carolina, Georgia, and Florida before the regiment transfers to Virginia to fight with Lee's Army of Northern Virginia in 1864. He serves there as a teamster. The regiment's muster roll lists Dodd as "Absent with Leave." LOC

Private Eli Franklin (left) enlists in Company B, 1st South Carolina Infantry, at Newberry, South Carolina, on July 7, 1861. He only suffers a single wound during the entire war. On August 10, 1864, he is admitted to a hospital in Charlottesville, Virginia, with "Coutusis [sic] left thigh"—which means a contusion on the left thigh, likely caused by a piece of shrapnel or spent bullet, neither of which penetrated the skin. LOC

Sergeant Berry Benson (left) enlists in the 1st (McCreary's) South Carolina Infantry in August 1861 and is wounded during the spring of 1863. (The nature of his wound and the battle in which he is wounded is not recorded.) He returns to his unit that fall. Benson is captured at Spotsylvania Court House on May 17, 1864, and shipped to Washington's Old Capitol Prison before being transferred to Elmira prison in New York. There, Benson joins a group of prisoners digging a 66-foot escape tunnel. At 4:00 AM on October 7, 1864, he and nine other prisoners escape. Traveling alone, Benson walks all the way to New Market, Virginia, where he is given a pass to rejoin his unit near Petersburg. Benson surrenders at Appomattox Court House. *LOC*

Confederate cavalrymen supplied their own mounts. When **R. Cecile Johnson** (right) transfers from the 8th Georgia to the Hampton Legion Cavalry Battalion in September 1861, his horse is valued at just $19.20. He dies in the fight at Upperville, Virginia, on June 21, 1863. *LOC*

Before the Civil War, a number of state militia units modeled themselves after the French Zouaves. The fancy uniforms and pageantry of parades prompt many young men to join. **Ellis Green** (right) is a member of the McCellan Zouaves, a South Carolina militia unit. The McCellan Zouaves serves in Charleston, South Carolina, from January 1861 to January 1862. The dull routine of drill, guarding prisoners, and building fortifications does not appeal to many of the Zouaves, so when the unit undergoes a reorganization in early 1862, there are not enough volunteers and the unit is dissolved. Private Green may have enlisted in a cavalry unit. LOC

Henry Timrod (left) is one of the country's best-known poets of the Civil War era. In "A Cry to Arms," Timrod calls for Southern men to leave their work and join the Confederate Army. He takes his own advice and enlists in Company B, 20th South Carolina Infantry, but spends most of his military career on "detached service." His time in the ranks is brief and he is discharged on December 8, 1862, for tuberculosis. The disease claims his life in 1867. LOC

Disabled soldiers are often assigned light duty to free up healthy men for combat. **Alphonso Ebenezer Gettys** (left) is about 18 when he enlists in the 5th South Carolina Infantry. In September 1862 he loses one or more fingers when a sliding door on a railroad car closes on them. After a short stay in the 5th Division Hospital at Richmond, he is granted a 30-day furlough. When he returns, Gettys is assigned as a nurse in the division hospital. When Richmond falls in April 1865, he travels west with what is left of Lee's Army of Northern Virginia and surrenders on April 9 at Appomattox Court House. *Melvin Ware*

After the war, Alphonso Gettys returns to York County, South Carolina, and takes up farming. In 1868, he marries his 20-year-old first cousin **Sarah Templeton**. The loss of his finger(s) did not affect his ability to farm or do manual labor, for he is able to lift a bale of cotton by himself. *Melvin Ware*

Sergeant Sumner A. Cunningham (right) enlists in the 41st Tennessee Infantry in April 1861. Captured when Fort Donelson surrenders in February 1862, he is held at Camp Morton, Indiana, until exchanged. Cunningham is hospitalized near Chattanooga in October 1864, but returns to his unit in time to fight at and survive the bloody Battle of Franklin in Tennessee in November 1864. In 1893, Cunningham publishes the first issue of *Confederate Veteran*, a magazine for and about former Southern soldiers. His work produces a tremendous body of history for future scholars of the war. LOC

James Bishop White (left) is 24 when he musters into the 60th Tennessee Mounted Infantry at Hayesville, Tennessee. He is promoted to first sergeant on March 18, 1863, but has little time to enjoy his promotion before being captured, along with most of his regiment, at the Battle of Big Black River outside Vicksburg less than two months later. White is confined at Point Lookout and Fort Delaware before being exchanged near the end of the war in early 1865. LOC

Seventeen-year-old **Henry Howe Cook** (left) enlists in the 1st Tennessee Infantry on May 9, 1861. The teenager is assigned to assist the wagon master as a teamster. Promoted to lieutenant, the young officer is next assigned to the 44th Tennessee on December 21, 1861. Lt. Cook is shot in the hand at the Battle of Murfreesboro (Stones River) at the end of 1862 and is later captured at Drewry's Bluff outside Richmond on May 16, 1864. Cook becomes one of the Immortal Six Hundred—Confederate officers used as human shields by Federal forces in Charleston Harbor. He survives the war. *LOC*

Blacksmith **Thomas Bowen** (right) is in his 60s when he joins the Zollicoffer Mounted Rifles, a home guard unit, in eastern Tennessee. Union raiders kill him on his farm in April 1865. *Terry Bowen*

Bowie knife-wielding 35-year-old **Private Thomas F. Bates** (right) of the 6th Texas Infantry looks ready for action, but he never sees combat. He is reported "absent sick" during much of the summer of 1862 and is discharged by a Surgeon's Certificate of Disability before October 1862. *LOC*

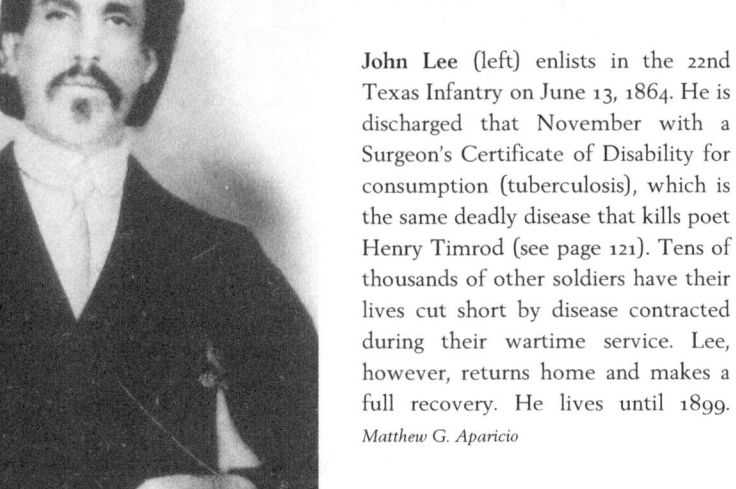

John Lee (left) enlists in the 22nd Texas Infantry on June 13, 1864. He is discharged that November with a Surgeon's Certificate of Disability for consumption (tuberculosis), which is the same deadly disease that kills poet Henry Timrod (see page 121). Tens of thousands of other soldiers have their lives cut short by disease contracted during their wartime service. Lee, however, returns home and makes a full recovery. He lives until 1899. *Matthew G. Aparicio*

Sergeant James Robert Box (left) enlists in Company D, 14th Texas Cavalry, on July 1, 1862. His horse is valued at $200.00 and his equipment at $25.00. Since the regiment fights as infantry, it is often referred to as the 14th Texas (Dismounted) Cavalry. The regiment fights in Kentucky, Mississippi, Tennessee, Georgia, and Alabama. Box is captured in April 1865 at the Battle of Spanish Fort, Alabama, part of the Mobile operations. Sergeant Box is confined at Ship Island, Mississippi, before being paroled at Meridian, Mississippi, on May 11, 1865. *Jack R. Box*

Twenty-nine-year old **Private John Simmons** (right) enlists in the 22nd Texas Infantry in March of 1862. Before the war ends, he sees action in Louisiana at Milliken's Bend during the Vicksburg campaign, and at Mansfield (Sabine Crossroads) and Pleasant Hill during the Red River campaign. Simmons's regiment, part of John Walker's Texas Division, then moves into Arkansas to confront Union Maj. Gen. Frederick Steele's expedition and fights at Jenkins' Ferry. During the war Simmons writes more than 80 letters home to his wife Nancy. *Barbara Beadles*

The twin 16-year-old Moore brothers, **John C. and William Savage**, enlist in Parker's Company of Light Artillery on March 14, 1862. The boys did not have their mother's permission to enlist, so she begins a letter-writing campaign to have them discharged. In addition to pointing out her sons enlisted without her consent, she also claims they are in ill health. The boys are discharged on October 8, 1862. John's brief enlistment may have quenched his desire to serve in the Confederate Army, and there is no record of a John C. Moore serving in another unit from Virginia. William's brief service, however, whets his appetite for military service and in 1864, the 18-year-old enlists in the 1st Company of Howitzers, Virginia Light Artillery Battery. William is promoted to second lieutenant and transfers to Company I, 15th Virginia Infantry, on March 27, 1865. Within a week he is promoted to captain. William is wounded in the left arm on April 2 and taken prisoner, and confined in a hospital at Washington, D.C. He is released after signing an Oath of Allegiance to the United States. *LOC*

Sergeant John W. Anthony of the 11th Virginia Infantry (left) fights at Manassas (Bull Run) on July 20, 1861. Confederates can pay a substitute to take their place in the army, so he furnishes one on February 26, 1862. The substitute, however, goes AWOL before the end of the month, and Anthony returns to his unit. He is wounded at Seven Pines on May 31, 1862. In April 1865 he is treated for a severe wound in his right thigh suffered at Petersburg. Anthony recovers and lives until 1920. *LOC*

Sergeant James W. Millner (right), shown here with a bayonet on his musket, a holstered pistol, and a large knife, enlists in Company K, 38th Virginia Infantry, in June of 1861. He is slightly wounded at the Battle of Malvern Hill on July 1, 1862, while the 38th Virginia is part of Lewis Armistead's brigade. The following January Millner resigns his rank and serves the rest of the war as a private. He suffers a more serious wound in the neck at the Battle of Five Forks on April 1, 1865, but survives the war. *LOC*

Many soldiers have problems adjusting to the rules and regimentation of army life. **David C. Colbert** (left) enlists in the 46th Virginia Infantry in 1861 and finds himself on "guard report" three times in 1862 for violating regulations. The 46th Virginia sees action in the Seven Days' Battles, the siege of Charleston, South Carolina, and around Petersburg. Colbert is captured during the retreat to Appomattox at Farmville, Virginia, on April 6, 1865. *LOC*

Private Edward A. Carey of Company I, 44th Virginia Infantry, poses here with his married sister **Emma Carey Garland**. Carey is killed in action early in the war at Port Republic, Virginia, on June 9, 1862. His effects, valued at $25.68, are given to his brother William who serves in the same company. *LOC*

Private Peter Lauck Kurtz (right) of the 5th Virginia Infantry is promoted to sergeant in April 1862 and absent sick most of that fall. He is captured at Fisher's Hill in the Shenandoah Valley in Virginia on September 2, 1864. The next month Kurtz transfers to the Quartermaster Corps, which is responsible for supplying the armies in the field. Quartermaster Sergeant Kurtz surrenders at Appomattox Court House. *LOC*

Theophilus Mann (left) enlists in Company G, 1st (Farinholt's) Virginia Infantry Battalion Reserves in May of 1864. He is detailed from December 21, 1864 to April 1, 1865, for "private necessity." The record does not explain the nature of Mann's "necessity." *LOC*

Bernard B. Graves (right) joins the Nelson's Company, Virginia Light Artillery (Hanover Artillery) May 22, 1861. In October of 1862, he transfers to Kilpatrick's Company, Virginia Light Artillery (Amherst Artillery) and fights with it the rest of the war (part of the time as a corporal) at Gettysburg, Cold Harbor, and with Jubal Early in the Shenandoah Valley. Graves is captured near Waynesboro, Virginia, on March 2, 1865, held at Fort Delaware, and released in June 1865. Graves died at the age of 43. *LOC*

A handwritten note accompanying this ambrotype identifies this soldier as **Tomley Lumpkin** (right) of Company K, 34th Virginia Infantry, who is killed in the Civil War. The company records do not list a "Tomley" Lumpkin, but four men with the same Lumpkin surname serve in the company: **Bolivar Lumpkin** is wounded and "left on the battlefield" at Seven Pines (Fair Oaks) Virginia on May 31, 1862. He is eventually transported to Crow's Factory Hospital and dies there on June 21, 1862; **Cincinnatus Lumpkin** transfers to the Confederate States Navy; **Henry T. Lumpkin** dies of Pyemia (infection) at Petersburg, Virginia, on September 13, 1864; **Theodore F. Lumpkin** is captured at Petersburg, Virginia, on June 16, 1864 and held at Elmira, New York, and Point Lookout, Maryland, before he is exchanged on October 14, 1864. *LOC*

John Richard Whitehead (left) of the 6th Virginia Cavalry. Promoted to first sergeant in September of 1862 and captured at the cavalry fight at Brandy Station in June 1863. Whitehead is held at Old Capitol Prison in Washington, exchanged, and detailed to "gather horses." The cavalryman is shot in his right side during the Spotsylvania Court House operation in May 1864 and hospitalized in Richmond's Chimborazo Hospital. During a 60-day furlough he marries Sallie Hunt Graves. He returns to his unit and is once again detailed to "horse duty." After the war, Whitehead serves as sheriff and then county treasurer of Pittsylvania County, Virginia. *Fletcher B. Watson, IV*

Charles B. Mosby (left) is just 13 when he enlists as a drummer in the 6th Virginia Infantry in June of 1861, and reported AWOL in April 1862, discharged from the army because he is a minor. That November he enlists as a drummer in Company B of Henderson's (Virginia) Heavy Artillery. This time Mosby stays with his company until he is transferred to play in the battery's band. *LOC*

Drum Major Carl R. M. Pohle (right) organizes Drum Major Carl R. M. Pohle's Drum Corps in May 1861. The unit, part of the 1st Virginia Infantry, soon discards its fancy uniforms for more practical clothing. The 40-year-old Pohle is ill and on furlough in October 1861. No further records of Drum Major Pohle have been located. *LOC*

Private David Lowry (right) pulls several disappearing acts during the war. The private, whose surname is also spelled "Lowery," is a member of the 41st Virginia Militia, but "removed from the county" before it went into service. He next enlists in the 25th Virginia Mounted Rifles on September 18, 1861, but that December is listed as "Absent Without Leave since enlisting in the 37th Virginia Infantry without transfer." The 37th Virginia is fighting under Maj. Gen. Thomas J. "Stonewall" Jackson in the Shenandoah Valley when Lowry is captured at Kernstown, Virginia, on March 23, 1862. After his exchange in August 1862, he disappears for a final time when he does not return to his regiment, which lists him AWOL once more. *LOC*

Thomas Garland Jefferson (left) is a great-great-nephew of the third president, Thomas Jefferson, and a cadet at the Virginia Military Institute when he is shot in the chest at the Battle of New Market on May 15, 1864. He lingers three days before succumbing to his wound. Jefferson is one of six of the ten cadets killed or mortally wounded at New Market who are buried beneath the statue "Virginia Mourning her Dead" on the VMI campus. *Virginia Military Institute*

Moses Ezekiel (left), who creates the Virginia Mourning her Dead statue at VMI, also fights at New Market with the VMI Corps of Cadets. Ezekiel later serves with the Corps of Cadets in the trenches at Richmond during the siege. After the war he goes to Europe and works as a world famous sculptor. Ezekiel dies in 1917 and is buried in Arlington National Cemetery. Ironically, he lies near the Confederate monument, which he considered his greatest work. *Virginia Military Institute*

Private Luther Hart Clapp (right) spends much of his time in the 37th Virginia Infantry as a patient in Virginia hospitals. Clapp enlists in May 1861, and the next year is "transferred to the Kentucky Cavalry by order of the Secretary of War." No record of his serving in any Kentucky cavalry unit has been located. *LOC*

Sixteen-year-old **William T. Biedler** (left) serves as a sergeant in Company C, Mosby's Rangers (43rd Virginia Battalion), the most famous partisan unit of the war. Major John S. Mosby (the "Grey Ghost") organizes it on June 10, 1863, and launches hit-and-run raids in northern Virginia before blending back into the civilian population of what becomes known as "Mosby's Confederacy." Biedler is holding an old flintlock musket. He survives the war and eventually moves to Maryland, where he dies on July 8, 1897 at age 51. *LOC*

Private Lucien Love (right) serves in Company D of Mosby's Rangers. Although he is shown with a sword, the six-shot revolver was the weapon of choice for most of Mosby's men. Guerrilla units like Mosby's do not keep records. Little is known about their actions during the war. *LOC*

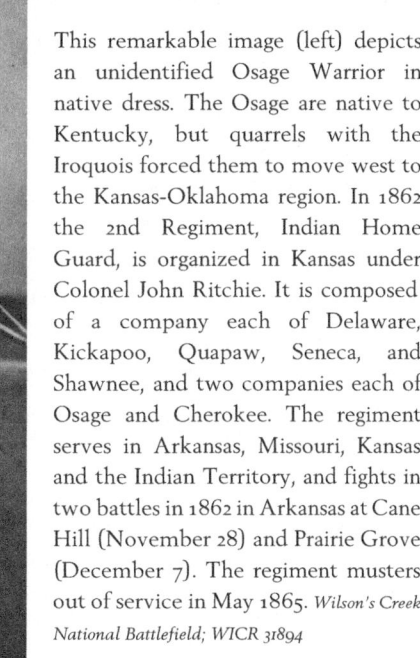

This remarkable image (left) depicts an unidentified Osage Warrior in native dress. The Osage are native to Kentucky, but quarrels with the Iroquois forced them to move west to the Kansas-Oklahoma region. In 1862 the 2nd Regiment, Indian Home Guard, is organized in Kansas under Colonel John Ritchie. It is composed of a company each of Delaware, Kickapoo, Quapaw, Seneca, and Shawnee, and two companies each of Osage and Cherokee. The regiment serves in Arkansas, Missouri, Kansas and the Indian Territory, and fights in two battles in 1862 in Arkansas at Cane Hill (November 28) and Prairie Grove (December 7). The regiment musters out of service in May 1865. *Wilson's Creek National Battlefield; WICR 31894*

To the Last Man: The Final Confederate Soldier

When Walter Williams died in December 1959, he was widely reported as the last surviving Confederate veteran. In its January 11, 1960, issue, *Life Magazine* reports Williams's death in an article written by noted Civil War historian Bruce Catton entitled "The End of the Gallant Rebs."

Several historians dispute Williams's claim of service in the Confederate Army. These researchers uses census records, pension applications, and surviving Confederate military records to attempt to name the last Confederate soldier. Some historians question the accuracy of the 1860 Federal Census because it is taken by Federal marshals in states that were on the brink of leaving the Union. These researchers believe many men who are old enough to serve in the military are not reported. While most Confederate records survive the war, many do not. These missing records make it difficult to disprove a man's claim of service in the Confederate Army.

In a 1991 article in *Blue and Gray Magazine* called "The Great Imposters," William Marvel examines several men who claim to be the last surviving Confederate soldier. According to Marvel, Williams is born between October 1854 and April 1855 in Itawamba County, Mississippi. If these dates are correct, Williams is too young to have served in the Confederate Army.

In his book *Lee's Last Retreat: The Flight to Appomattox* (Chapel Hill, 2002), Marvel concludes Pleasant Crump of Talladega County, Alabama, who dies on December 31, 1951, is the last confirmed surviving Confederate veteran. Marvel explains that, after Crump's death, at least twelve others claim to be former Confederate soldiers. Marvel relies heavily on census records to disprove their claims. *In The Last Civil War Veterans: The Lives of the Final Survivors State by State* (McFarland, 2016), author Frank L. Gryzb agrees Pleasant Crump is the last survivor whose war service can be proven.

The books and articles mentioned above are recommended for readers who wish to read more on this sidelight of the war.

Researching Your Confederate Ancestor

Some records are removed from Richmond before the city falls in 1865, but many are lost in the fire that sweeps through much of the commercial heart of the Southern capital. Surviving records, with other documents captured or donated by individuals are held by the U.S. War Department.

In 1903, the War Department begins creating Complied Service Records (CSRs) for Confederate soldiers. Information from sources including muster rolls, hospital registers, casualty lists, receipts, and prison records are recorded on cards for each man, put in an envelope, and filed. Some CSRs records contain letters, paroles, and other records specific to that soldier's experience. CSRs vary. Typically, more information exists for soldiers who served in the Eastern Theater than elsewhere, and for records covering the first two or three years of the conflict. The majority of the information on the soldiers highlighted in this book, for example, comes from Complied Service Records.

In 1938, the records are sent to the National Archives in Washington and are eventually microfilmed. Researchers may view the microfilm at the archives, or order copies of a soldier's Complied Service Record from the archives: www.archives.gov. Broadfoot Publishing (www.broadfootpublishing.com) sells copies of Confederate compiled service records. Fold 3 (www.fold3.com) is a subscription service for searching and downloading CSRs.

To order a CSR you must know the unit(s) in which he served. The National Park Service's Civil War Soldiers and Sailors System online database is covers both sides: www.nps.gov/civilwar/soldiers-and-sailors-data base.htm. A search will return the man's unit and rank. The records of Union and Confederate sailors were never compiled. At present this online database includes only the names of some 18,000 African-American sailors who served in the Union Navy.

Many state archives hold microfilmed Complied Service Records for Confederate units raised in their state. Some public libraries also hold microfilm for Confederate units recruited from their service area.

The National Archives also holds three more Confederate CSR records:

(1) Compiled Service Records of Confederate Soldiers Who Served in Organizations Raised Directly by the Confederate Government has records of men who served in the Confederate Cavalry and units of Native Americans;

(2) Compiled Service Records of Confederate General and Staff Officers, and Non-Regimental Enlisted Men has the records of men who served in units such as the Quartermaster Corps and Medical Corps. The Civil War Soldiers and Sailors System will return the names of men whose records are in both of these if no state is entered when a man's name is entered on the search page.;

(3) Unfiled Papers and Slips Belonging to Confederate Compiled Service Records consists of 442 rolls of microfilm of records that were never filed in soldiers' Complied Service Records. This series, which is indexed on microfilm, is available at the National Archives and some of its regional branches.

States provided pensions for Confederate veterans and widows and their archives hold this information. Not all former Confederate states loaned material to develop CSRs. This material may be researched in these state archives. CSRs were not created for home guard or state militia units that were not mustered into Confederate service. State archives may hold information on men who served in units organized in their state.

Some Confederate prisoners joined the Union Army. These "Galvanized Yankees" were organized into six regiments of US Volunteers. The CSRs of United States Volunteers have not been microfilmed. Copies of these records may be ordered from the National Archives.

The Federal government spent four million dollars burying Union soldiers; most dead Confederate soldiers were buried (or re-buried) by Southern Ladies' Memorial Associations. Burial sites for Confederates have never been compiled. (The author's *Confederate Cemeteries* series lists burials in 80 Virginia cemeteries.) Congress appointed a commissioner in 1906 to locate and mark Confederate graves (including civilians) in Union prisons. The 1912 report *Register of Soldiers, Sailors & Citizens of the Confederacy Who Died in Northern Prisons & Hospitals* lists the names and burial locations of more than 25,500. The register, National Archives microfilm #M918, may be ordered from the National Archives. Some public libraries hold copies of the microfilm.

One often-overlooked source of material about Confederate soldiers is the books written by other soldiers who served in the same unit as the man you are researching. The soldiers who wrote these accounts often discussed their comrades, and their insights include everything from the mundane of camp life to fighting in battles and much more—topics that are not always found in other official records. A search on Google Books may reveal many worthwhile publications.

In addition to checking with various state or local archives, various lineage societies, such as the Church of Latter Day Saints genealogy site: www.familysearch.org are often worthwhile.

For other digitized records, visit your public library or subscription-based websites like www.ancestry.com or www.findagrave.com.

The multi-volume *Official Records of the War of Rebellion*, published after the war, has an extensive index and almost certainly significant information on the unit in which your ancestor served, and perhaps even information about your ancestor. Don't overlook it.

In addition, newspapers are often a rich and overlooked source for information as many Confederate soldiers wrote articles during and after the war that appeared in the papers.

Glossary of Civil War Terms

Abatis: A defensive work consisting of a series of felled trees, their ends sharpened and pointed toward the enemy.

Abolitionist: A person who advocates the abolishment, or ending, of slavery.

Anaconda Plan: General Winfield Scott's strategic plan to quell the rebellion, calling for a blockade of southern ports and occupation of the Mississippi River—squeezing the Confederate states into submission like a giant snake, or anaconda.

Anti-Slavery: A person who was against the spread of slavery, but not necessarily in favor of its abolition in places where it already existed.

Artillery: A term used to describe large-caliber guns, or cannon, as well as the branch of service that operated such weapons.

Blue Belly: A term for Union soldiers derived from the slang "yellowbelly" or coward.

Bounty: Money paid by states and the Federal government to entice men to enlist in the Union armed forces. Bounties ranged from $300.00 to over $700.00. Early in the War, the Confederacy offered $50.00 bounties.

Bounty Jumper: A person who joined the Union armed forces, collected an enlistment bounty, deserted, and repeated the process. Some "Bounty Jumpers" joined as many as half-a-dozen units during the course of the war.

Breastwork: A temporary defensive work erected to protect troops from enemy fire, often constructed in haste out of available materials, such as earth and felled trees.

Brevet: A temporary or honorary rank, often granted for meritorious service during war, which did not carry the authority or pay of a full rank.

Canister: An artillery projectile consisting of small iron or lead balls packed with sawdust into a tin can, or canister, which scattered upon firing, acting like a shotgun blast. Normally fired against attacking infantry, canister rounds had an effective range of 100 to 400 yards.

Carpetbaggers: A term for Northerners who went South during Reconstruction in search of financial gain, derived from the carpet bags used for carrying their belongings.

Caisson: A horse-drawn wagon or chest that carried ammunition for field artillery.

Chevaux-de-frise: A wooden frame (often a single log) embedded with crossed wooden spikes, pointed toward the enemy. Often used to fill gaps in a defensive line.

Christian Commission: A massive volunteer organization that provided aid to Union soldiers during the war, from reading material to medical supplies and treatment.

Contraband: A term used to describe fugitive slaves who came into Union lines during the war. These ex-slaves were considered contrabands of war by U.S. officials because their labor aided the Southern war effort.

Copperheads: Northern Democrats opposed to the war. Also referred to as "Peace Democrats," they advocated an immediate peace settlement with the Confederacy. Many were imprisoned after Abraham Lincoln suspended the right of habeas corpus.

Defilade: A position protected from enemy fire or observation by a natural or manmade barrier.

Demonstration: A secondary or threatened attack designed to deceive the enemy. Demonstrations were made against a portion of the enemy's line away from the target of the main attack.

Earthwork: A defensive work erected to protect troops from enemy fire, often consisting of series of trenches.

Emancipation Proclamation: A Presidential order, preliminarily issued September 22, 1862, freeing all slaves in states still in rebellion as of January 1, 1863. Slaves in the border states (Delaware, Kentucky, Maryland, Missouri) were exempted. Paved the way for ex-slaves to enter the U.S. Army and Navy.

Enfilade: Gunfire directed along an enemy's battle line from a flanking position, producing maximum damage with minimum exposure.

Flank: The end of an army's line in battle, or a type of attack directed at an enemy's flank (i.e., a flanking maneuver).

Furlough: Leave granted enlisted men, often the sick or wounded.

Galvanized Yankees: Confederate prisoners of war who swore allegiance to the United States and joined the Union army. The six regiments of Galvanized Yankees raised were sent west to fight Indians.

Grand Army of the Republic: The politically powerful fraternal organization of Union veterans of the war, founded in 1866. Often referred to as 'the GAR.'

Grape Shot: An artillery projectile filled with iron balls held together by iron plates and rings, largely superceded by the start of the war by canister.

Greybacks: 1. Lice. 2. Union troops' slang term for Confederates, derived from their grey uniforms.

Guerrilla: A term for civilians who engaged in warfare, or for the hit-and-run tactics they employed.

Hardtack: A hard wheat biscuit, 3 by 3 inches, issued as rations to troops, who regularly derided it as inedible.

Haversack: A small, durable bag in which soldiers carried personal belongings; often slung over one shoulder.

Invalid Corps: A reserve command established in 1863 consisting of Union soldiers (both on active service or recently discharged) too disabled to serve in combat but capable of performing other light military duties (e.g., provost guard, nursing, cooking, garrison duty). Renamed the Veterans Reserve Corp (VRC) in 1864, over 60,000 men served in its ranks during the war.

Ironclad: A warship covered (clad) with iron plating; all Civil War ironclads were steam powered.

Legion: A regiment consisting of infantry, cavalry, and artillery companies.

Minie Ball: A cone-shaped lead bullet, designed by and named after Captain Claude-Etienne Minié of the French army, used in rifled muskets. The bullet's hollow based expanded upon firing, forcing it into the grooves (or rifling) inside the gun's barrel. As a result, the bullet spun as it exited the barrel, stabilizing it in flight and resulting in increased range and accuracy.

Mortar: A large but short-barreled artillery piece designed to lob explosive shells at a high arc toward enemy positions. Used most often during siege operations. The war's largest mortar, called the Dictator, sent 200-lb. explosive shells a distance of approximately 2 ½ miles.

Parole: Status of prisoners of war released on their personal assurance that they would not again take up arms until formally exchanged.

Picket: A soldier on guard, often beyond the main lines. A group of pickets, or a picket line, was often employed to guard against a surprise enemy attack.

Pontoon: A low, flat-bottomed wooden boat. Pontoon bridges—dozens to hundreds of pontoons strung together and covered with wooden boards— allowed advancing armies to cross various bodies of water in short order.

Quaker Gun: A log painted to resemble a cannon to fool the enemy. The name apparently stemmed from the Quakers' opposition to war.

Ram: A stream-powered ship with an iron ram attached to its bow, designed to sink enemy ships via collision.

Sanitary Commission: A federal government agency created in 1861 to coordinate the volunteer efforts of women during the war. Female volunteers organized fundraisers, staffed hospitals, and sewed uniforms, among countless other activities.

Scalawag: A white Southerner who supported Republican efforts during Reconstruction.

Secesh: Shorthand for "secessionist," or a person who advocated the secession of southern states in 1860-1861 or supported the Confederate war effort.

Siege: Military tactic by which an enemy force is surrounded, preventing its re-supply and forcing it into eventual surrender.

Skedaddle: Slang often employed by soldiers referring to a hasty withdrawal or retreat.

Skirmish: Light combat, often entailing an exchange of fire between opposing pickets or other advanced forces.

Sutler: A civilian merchant authorized to sell miscellaneous goods (e.g., tobacco, books, food) to soldiers. Sutlers followed the armies in horse-drawn carts, setting up shop when the armies camped.

Torpedo: Name describing any one of a variety of exploding mines employed during the war, both on land and in sea.

USCT: United States Colored Troops, regiments of the U.S. Army that consisted of black soldiers and white officers.

Veterans Reserve Corps: See Invalid Corps.

Zouave: Union or Confederate outfit modeled after French Zouaves, distinguished by their colorful uniforms, including baggy trousers and turbans or fezzes.

Civil War Points of Interest

Whether searching for a Civil War site in your area or planning an extended Civil War-themed trip, the following list of sites will get you started. All contact information—including websites, where available—was current at the time of publication. Operating hours vary, so please check ahead before hitting the road.

*   *   *

Alabama

Confederate Memorial Park
437 County Road 63, Marbury, Alabama 36051
(205) 755-1990 / ahc.alabama.gov/properties/confederate/confederate.aspx
Two cemeteries/museum tell the story of Alabama's Confederate Soldiers' Home.

Fort Gaines Historic Site
51 Bienville Boulevard, Dauphin Island, Alabama 36528
(251) 861-6992 / www.dauphinisland.org/fort.htm
Fort Gaines protected Mobile Bay from Union attack during the Civil War.

Fort Morgan State Historic Site
51 Highway 180 West, Gulf Shores, Alabama 36542
(334) 540-7125 / www.fort-morgan.org/
Commemorates Adm. David Farragut and Battle of Mobile Bay.

Arkansas

Arkansas Post National Memorial
1741 Old Post Road, Gillett, Arkansas 72055
870-548-2207 / www.nps.gov/arpo/index.htm
Preserves the site of Fort Hindman, built by Confederates in 1862 and captured by Federal forces in 1863. The earthen structure has since been destroyed by erosion.

Jenkins Ferry State Park
Located 13 miles south of Sheridan on Ark. 46. (No staff on site.)
www.arkansasstateparks.com/park-finder/parks.aspx?id=28
Part of the failed Red River campaign, where Federals held off Confederate attacks.

Marks' Mills State Park
Located southeast of Fordyce at the junction of Ark. 97 and Ark. 8
888-AT-PARKS / www.arkansasstateparks.com/marksmills/
Red River campaign, April 1864; Confederates captured 220 wagons.

Pea Ridge National Military Park
15930 E. Highway 62, Garfield, Arkansas 72732
(479) 451-8122 / www.nps.gov/peri/
Several thousand Native Americans fought with the Confederates at Elkhorn Tavern (Pea Ridge). The Union won and kept Missouri in the Union.

Poison Spring State Park
Located 10 miles west of Camden on Ark. 76
888-AT-PARKS / www.arkansasstateparks.com/poisonspring/
Part of Red River campaign,. were Confederates ambushed Union supply train.

Prairie Grove Battlefield State Park
506 East Douglas Street, Prairie Grove, Arkansas 72753
(479) 846-2990 / www.arkansasstateparks.com/prairiegrovebattlefield/
This December 1862 battle was the last major engagement in northeastern Arkansas.

Colorado

Sand Creek Massacre National Historic Site
35110 Highway 194 E., La Junta, Colorado 81050
(719) 438-5916 / www.nps.gov/sand/index.htm
Late 1864, Col. John Chivington attacked Cheyenne Chief Black Kettle's village.

District of Columbia

Ford's Theatre National Historic Site
511 10th Street NW, Washington, D.C. 20004
(202) 233-0701 / www.nps.gov/foth/
John Wilkes Booth assassinated Abraham Lincoln here on April 14, 1865. The president died the next morning, across the street in the Petersen House.

Fort Circle Parks
Located at various sites in and around the city.
www.nps.gov/cwdw/index.htm
View remnants of several forts erected to defend the capital during the war.

Lincoln's Cottage at the Soldiers' Home
140 Rock Creek Church Road NW, Washington, D.C. 20011
(202) 829-0436 / www.lincolncottage.org/index.htm
Lincoln and his family lived here for long stretches of time during the war.

Florida

Gulf Islands National Seashore—Gulf Breeze
1801 Gulf Breeze Parkway, Gulf Breeze, Florida 32563
(850) 934-2600 / www.nps.gov/guis/index.htm
Civil War-era Forts Barrancas, Pickens, Massachusetts, and McRee.

Natural Bridge Battlefield Historic State Park
7502 Natural Bridge Road, Tallahassee, Florida 32305
(850) 922-6007 / www.floridastateparks.org/naturalbridge/default.cfm
Confederates turned back a Federal advance here on March 6, 1865.

Olustee Battlefield Historic State Park
P.O. Box 40, Olustee, Florida 32072
(386) 758-0400 / www.floridastateparks.org/olustee/default.cfm
The February 1864 battle in which U.S. Colored Troops regiments participated.

Georgia

Andersonville National Historic Site
496 Cemetery Road, Andersonville, Georgia 31711
(229) 924-0343 / www.nps.gov/ande/
The largest Confederate-run POW camp; some 12,000 Union soldiers perished.

Augusta Canal National Heritage Area
1450 Greene Street, Augusta, GA 30901, (706) 823-0440
Interprets Augusta's role in the war, and the site of the Augusta Powder Works.

Chickamauga and Chattanooga National Military Park
Fort Oglethorpe, Georgia 30742
(706) 866-9241 / www.nps.gov/chch/
The nation's first national military park preserves the site of the only major Southern
victory in the Western Theater, one of the largest battles of the war.

Fort McAllister Historic Park
3894 Fort McAllister Road, Richmond Hill, Georgia 31324
(912) 727-2339 / gastateparks.org/info/ftmcallister/
The Confederates defeated many naval attacks but fell to ground forces in 1864.

Fort Pulaski National Monument—Tybee Island
Savannah, Georgia 31410
(912) 786-5787 / www.nps.gov/fopu/
Pulaski guarded the water approach to Savannah. In April 1862, U.S. rifled cannon battered the fort into submission in less than two days.

Jefferson Davis Memorial Historic Site
338 Jeff Davis Park Road, Fitzgerald, Georgia 31750
(229) 831-2335 / https://gastateparks.org/JeffersonDavisMemorial
A monument and museum mark the site were Union forces captured the Confederate president on May 9, 1865.

Kennesaw Mountain National Battlefield Park
900 Kennesaw Mountain Drive, Kennesaw, Georgia 30152
(770) 427-4686 / www.nps.gov/kemo/
At Kennesaw Mountain, Confederates foiled General William T. Sherman's attempt to break their lines during the campaign for Atlanta.

Pickett's Mill Battlefield Historic Site
4432 Mt. Tabor Church Road, Dallas, Georgia 30157
(770) 443-7850 / www.gastateparks.org/info/picketts/
Confederate defensive victory; one of the few preserved battlefields near Atlanta.

Illinois

Lincoln Home National Historic Site
413 South Eighth Street, Springfield, Illinois 62701-1905
(217) 391-3226 / www.nps.gov/liho/
President Lincoln lived here (1844 until he left for Washington in 1861).

Indiana

Lincoln Boyhood National Memorial
2916 E. South Street, Lincoln City, Indiana 47552
(812) 937-4541 / www.nps.gov/libo/
An interpretive site devoted to Lincoln's formative years in Indiana.

Kansas

Fort Scott National Historic Site
Fort Scott, Kansas 66701. (620) 223-0310 / www.nps.gov/fosc/index.htm
Fort Scott served as a Union supply depot during the war.

John Brown Museum
10th and Main Street, Osawatomie, Kansas 66064
(913) 755-4384 / www.kshs.org/places/johnbrown/index.htm
Visit the cabin where abolitionist John Brown lived, part of Underground Railroad.

Mine Creek Battlefield State Historic Site
20485 Kansas 52 Scenic, Pleasanton, Kansas 66075
(913) 352-8890 / www.kshs.org/places/minecreek/index.htm
On October 25, 1864, outnumbered Union cavalry defeated their counterparts here, capturing roughly 600 Confederates, including two generals.

Marais des Cygnes State Historic Site
26426 E 1700th Rd., Pleasanton, Kansas 66075
(913) 352-8890 / www.kshs.org/places/marais/index.htm
Site where free-state settlers were killed by pro-slavery settlers before the war.

Kentucky

Abraham Lincoln Birthplace National Historic Site
2995 Lincoln Farm Road, Hodgenville, Kentucky 42748
(270) 358-3137 / www.nps.gov/abli/index.htm
Abraham Lincoln was born here on February 12, 1809.

Columbus-Belmont State Park
350 Park Road, Columbus, Kentucky 42032
(270) 677-2327 / https://parks.ky.gov/parks/recreationparks/columbus-belmont/
U. S. Grant, in his first battle as a general, defeated Confederates in November 1861.

Jefferson Davis Monument State Historic Site
Highway 68 E, Fairview, Kentucky 42221
(270) 889-6100 / parks.ky.gov/findparks/histparks/jd/
Jefferson Davis was born here on June 3, 1808.

Perryville Battlefield State Historic Site
1825 Battlefield Road, Perryville, Kentucky 40468-0296
859-332-8631 / https://parks.ky.gov/parks/historicsites/perryville-battlefield/
Perryville ended General Bragg's 1862 Kentucky raid. The state stayed in the Union.

Louisiana

Camp Moore Confederate Cemetery and Museum
Hwy. 51, Tangipahoa, Louisiana
(985) 229-2438 / www.campmoorela.com/ Louisiana's largest CW training camp.

Centenary State Historic Site
3522 College St., Jackson, Louisiana 70748 / (225)634-7925
www.crt.state.la.us/louisiana-state-parks/historic-sites/centenary-state-historic-site/index
Both sides used the closed college as a hospital and headquarters during the war.

Confederate Memorial Hall Museum
929 Camp Str., New Orleans, LA, 70130 / (504) 523-4522
www.confederatemuseum.com / Houses the second-largest collection of Confederate Civil War items in the world. A magnificent must-see museum.

Fort Pike State Historic Site
27100 Chef Menteur Highway, New Orleans, Louisiana 70129
(504) 255-9171 / www.crt.state.la.us/parks/iFortpike.aspx
Confederates occupied the fort at the onset of war, but abandoned it when Federal troops took New Orleans. It became a training ground for USCT regiments.

Mansfield State Historic Site—Mansfield
15149 Highway 175, Mansfield, Louisiana 71052 / (318) 872-1474
www.crt.state.la.us/louisiana-state-parks/historic-sites/mansfield-state-historic-site/index
The Confederate victory that halted Nathaniel P. Banks's Red River Expedition.

Port Hudson State Historic Site—Jackson
236 Hwy 61, Jackson, Louisiana 70748 / (225) 654-3775
www.crt.state.la.us/louisiana-state-parks/historic-sites/port-hudson-state-historic-site
Port Hudson, the last Confederate fort on the Mississippi, fell after a 48-day siege.

Maryland

Antietam National Battlefield
302 E Main St., Sharpsburg, Maryland 21782
(301) 432-5124 / www.nps.gov/anti/
The Battle of Antietam, the bloodiest single-day battle of the war, marked the end of Robert E. lee's first invasion of the North.

Clara Barton National Historic Site
5801 Oxford Road, Glen Echo, Maryland 20812 / (301) 320-1410 / www.nps.gov/clba/ Visitors can tour the home of Clara Barton, Civil War nurse and founder of the American Red Cross.

Fort Washington Park
13551 Fort Washington Road, Fort Washington, Maryland 20744
(301) 763-4600 / www.nps.gov/fowa/index.htm
One of the many structures that guarded Washington, D.C., during the war.

Gathland State Park
21843 National Pike, Boonsboro, Maryland 21713
(301) 791-4767 / www.dnr.state.md.us/publiclands/western/gathland.html
Protects much of the 1862 South Mountain battle, prelude to Antietam.

Monocacy National Battlefield
5201 Urbana Pike, Frederick, Maryland 21704
(301) 662-3515 / www.nps.gov/mono/
Monocacy ("the battle that saved Washington") during Confederate General Jubal
Early's advance toward the capital in the summer of 1864.

National Museum of Civil War Medicine
48 E. Patrick Street, Frederick, Maryland 21705-0470
(301) 695-1864 / www.civilwarmed.org/
A wide array of medical programs and exhibits.

Michigan

Historic Fort Wayne
6325 W. Jefferson Ave., Detroit, Michigan 48209
(313) 628-0796 / www.historicfortwaynecoalition.com/
Established in 1845 and used as a place of induction to the U.S. military service.

Minnesota

Historic Fort Snelling
200 Tower Avenue, St. Paul, Minnesota 55111
(612) 725-1171 / www.historicfortsnelling.org/
Established in 1819 by Col. Josiah Snelling, who opened the area to homesteaders.

Wood Lake Battlefield
600th St. Echo, MN 56237
(507 280-9970 / www.woodlakebattlefield.com/
Site of a major engagement during the U.S.-Dakota war in 1862 when Minnesota had
its own civil war within the larger Civil War.

Fort Ridgely
82404 County Road 30, Fairfax, MN 55332

(507) 426-7888 / www.dnr.state.mn.us/state_parks/fort_ridgely/
Built in 1853 as a police station to keep peace as settlers poured into former Dakota lands. Withstood several attacks in the U.S.-Dakota War of 1862.

Mississippi

Beauvoir: The Jefferson Davis Home and Presidential Library
2244 Beach Blvd., Biloxi, Mississippi 39531
(228) 388-4400 / www.beauvoir.org/
Davis's final home was also a Confederate Veterans Home between 1903 and 1957.

Brices Cross Roads National Battlefield Site (No visitor center.)
Mississippi Hwy 370 near Baldwyn, Mississippi
Contact: Natchez Trace Parkway Visitor Center
(800) 305-7417 / / http://www.nps.gov/brcr/
On June 10, 1864, Major General Nathan Bedford Forrest's 3,500-man cavalry corps routed General Samuel D. Sturgis's 8,100 Union troops.

Grand Gulf Military Park
12006 Grand Gulf Road, Port Gibson, Mississippi 39150
(601) 437-5911 / www.grandgulfpark.state.ms.us/
A Confederate battery drove off Admiral Porter's ironclads, thwarting General Grant's plans to land troops.

Tupelo National Battlefield (No visitor center.)
Located on Main Street in Tupelo, Mississippi.
Contact: Natchez Trace Parkway Visitor Center
(800) 305-7417 / www.nps.gov/tupe/
Federal troops beat back Confederate attacks during this 1864 battle.

Vicksburg National Military Park
3201 Clay Street, Vicksburg, Mississippi 39183-3495
(601) 636-0583 / www.nps.gov/vick/
General Grant's siege and capture of Vicksburg helped split the Confederacy in two, opening the Mississippi River to Union shipping.

Missouri

Battle of Athens State Historic Site
Route 1, Box 26, Hwy CC, Revere, Missouri 63465
(660) 877-3871 / www.mostateparks.com/athens.htm
The northernmost Civil War battle fought west of the Mississippi.

Battle of Lexington State Historic Site
101 Delaware Street, Lexington, Missouri 64067
(660) 259-4654 / www.mostateparks.com/lexington/index.html
The restored Anderson House still shows damage inflicted by cannon balls fired during the "Battle of the Hemp Bales."

Confederate Memorial State Historic Site
211 West First Street, Higginsville, Missouri 64037
(660) 584-2853 / www.mostateparks.com/confedmem.htm
The Confederate Soldiers Home of Missouri opened in 1891 and housed 1,600 veterans and their families during its nearly 60 years of operation.

Ulysses S Grant National Historic Site
7400 Grant Road, St. Louis, Missouri 63123
(314) 842-3298 / www.nps.gov/ulsg/
Tour "White Haven," childhood home of Grant's wife, Julia Dent.

Wilson's Creek National Battlefield
6424 West Farm Road 182, Republic, Missouri 65738
(417) 732-2662 / www.nps.gov/wicr/
An 1861 Confederate victory in which Union General Nathaniel Lyon met his death.

New Mexico

Pecos National Historical Park
1 NM-63, Pecos, New Mexico 87552-0418
(505) 757-7200 / www.nps.gov/peco/
The 1862 Battle of Glorieta Pass ended the Confederate occupation of New Mexico.

North Carolina

Bennett Place
4409 Bennett Memorial Road, Durham, North Carolina 27705
(919) 383-4345 / www.nchistoricsites.org/Bennett/Bennett.htm
The restored farmhouse where Joe Johnston surrendered his army.

Bentonville Battlefield
5466 Harper House Road, Four Oaks, North Carolina 27524
(910) 594-0789 / www.nchistoricsites.org/Bentonvi/Bentonvi.htm
Bentonville represented the final Confederate attempt to stop Sherman's advance through North Carolina. Visitors may tour the 1850s Harper House, which was used as a field hospital after the battle.

CSS Neuse State Historic Site
2612 W. Vernon Avenue, Kinston, North Carolina 28502
(252) 522-2091 / https://historicsites.nc.gov/
Displays remnants of the salvaged ironclad gunboat CSS *Neuse*.

Fort Fisher State Historic Site
1610 Fort Fisher Blvd S., Kure Beach, North Carolina 28449
(910) 458-5538 / www.nchistoricsites.org/fisher/fisher.htm
Massive Fort Fisher fell on January 15, 1865, closing the Confederacy's largest remaining port at Wilmington, North Carolina.

Fort Macon State Park
2300 East Fort Macon Road, Atlantic Beach, North Carolina 28512
(252) 726-3775 / www.ncparks.gov/Visit/parks/foma/main.php
Confederates seized the fort in 1861; Union troops took it back in 1862.

Pennsylvania

Gettysburg National Military Park
1195 Baltimore Pike, Gettysburg, Pennsylvania 17325
(717) 334-1124 / www.nps.gov/gett/
The sprawling field covers much of the three-day battle at Gettysburg, which ended Robert E. Lee's second invasion of the North.

National Civil War Museum
One Lincoln Circle at Reservoir Park, Harrisburg, Pennsylvania 17105
(717) 260-1861 / www.nationalcivilwarmuseum.org/
A variety of exhibits tell the medical story of the war.

South Carolina

Fort Sumter National Monument
340 Concord Street, Charleston, South Carolina
www.nps.gov/fosu
The visitor center sheds light on the causes of the war and its outbreak here in April 1861. The fort itself is a separate entity; those wishing to visit it must do so by ferry.

Rivers Bridge State Historic Site
325 State Park Road, Ehrhardt, South Carolina 29081
(803) 267-3675 / www.southcarolinaparks.com/park-finder/state-park/566.aspx
For two days in early February 1865, outnumbered Confederates slowed Sherman's march through South Carolina at Rivers Bridge.

Tennessee

Carnton Plantation
1345 Carnton Lane, Franklin, Tennessee 37064
(615) 794-0903 / www.carnton.org/
The November 1864 Battle of Franklin swirled about John McGavock's plantation home, which served as a field hospital. After the war, the McGavock family put aside land to serve as a cemetery, in which some 1,500 Confederates are buried.

Carter House
1140 Columbia Ave., Franklin, Tennessee 37065
(615) 791-1861 / www.carterhouse1864.com/
A state-owned site preserving part of the Franklin battlefield where Confederate General John B. Hood attacked General John M. Schofield's Union army. Confederate Captain Theodrick Carter died died two days later here at his family's home.

Fort Donelson National Battlefield
120 Lock D Rd., Dover, Tennessee 37058
(931) 232-5348 / nps.gov/fodo/index.htm
The loss of Forts Henry and Donelson opened Tennessee to invasion.

Fort Pillow State Historic Park
3122 Park Road, Henning, Tennessee 38041
(731) 738-5581 / www.tennessee.gov/environment/parks/FortPillow/
On April 12, 1864, Gen. Nathan Bedford Forrest's Confederates overran the Union fort, killing 350 troops, many of them black, in what is widely regarded as a massacre.

Johnsonville State Historic Park
90 Redoubt Lane, New Johnsonville, Tennessee 37134
(931) 535-2789 / www.tennessee.gov/environment/parks/Johnsonville/
Massive supply depot attacked in November 1864 by Nathan Bedford Forrest's cavalry, which captured four Union gunboats and 14 steamboats.

Shiloh National Military Park
1055 Pittsburg Landing Road, Shiloh, Tennessee 38376
(731) 689-5696 / www.nps.gov/shil/
A Union victory, the two-day battle at Shiloh witnessed the death of the Confederate commander, Albert Sidney Johnston.

Stones River National Battlefield
3501 Old Nashville Highway, Murfreesboro, Tennessee 37129
(615) 893-9501 / www.nps.gov/stri/
A Federal victory that drove the Confederate army out of Middle Tennessee.

Texas

Sabine Pass Battleground State Historic Site
6100 Dowling Road, Port Arthur, Texas 77640
(512) 463-6323 / www.thc.state.tx.us/hsites/hs_sabine.aspx?Site=Sabine
A statue of Lt. Dick Dowling marks the site where he and 46 Confederates drove off
four Union gunboats and seven troop transports, saving East Texas from invasion.

Virginia

American Civil War Museum
1201 E. Clay Street, Richmond, Virginia 23219
(804) 649-1861 / www.acwm.org
The museum holds one of the largest collections of Confederate artifacts in the
country and the White House of the Confederacy.

Appomattox Court House National Historical Park
111 National Park Dr., Appomattox, Virginia 24522
(434) 352-8987 / www.nps.gov/apco/index.htm
View the McLean House, where General Lee surrendered in April 1865.

Arlington House, The Robert E. Lee Memorial
321 Sherman Dr, Fort Myer, VA 22211 (Arlington National Cemetery)
(703) 235-1530 / www.nps.gov/arho/index.htm
Arlington was Lee's home for 30 years. In 1861, the Lees fled south, never to return.

Cedar Creek & Belle Grove National Historical Park–Middletown and Strasburg
7712 Main Street, Middletown, Virginia 22645
(540) 869-30151 / www.nps.gov/cebe/index.htm
Preserves and interprets critical Shenandoah Valley battles.

Fredericksburg & Spotsylvania National Military Park
120 Chatham Lane, Fredericksburg, Virginia 22405
Www.nps.gov/frsp/index.htm
This remarkable park covers several battles, including Fredericksburg, Spotsylvania,
Chancellorsville, and smaller engagements.

Manassas National Battlefield Park
12521 Lee Highway, Manassas, Virginia 20109-2005
(703) 361-1339 / www.nps.gov/mana/index.htm
The Confederates won the first Battle of Manassas in 1861. A year later, the armies
met on the same ground, and the Confederates again prevailed.

Petersburg National Battlefield
1539 Hickory Hill Road, Petersburg, VA 23803
(804) 732-3531 / www.nps.gov/pete/index.htm
The 292-day Union siege of Petersburg cost some 20,000 Confederates their lives.

Richmond National Battlefield Park
3215 East Broad Street, Richmond, VA 23223
(804) 226-1981 / www.nps.gov/rich/index.htm
Tour many sites associated with Union attempts to capture the Southern capital.

Sailor's Creek Battlefield State Park
6541 Saylers Creek Road, Rice, Virginia 23966
(804) 561-7510 / www.dcr.virginia.gov/state_parks/sai.shtml
Where Union cavalry cut off about one-fourth of Lee's retreating army.

Staunton River Battlefield State Park
Randolph, VA 23962 (The park has two visitor centers)
Call for directions: (434) 454-4312 / www.stauntonriverbattlefield.org/
On June 25, 1864, 492 old men and young boys helped 296 Confederate reserves
defeat over 5,000 Union cavalrymen.

West Virginia

Carnifex Ferry Battlefield State Park
1194 Carnifex Ferry Road, Summersville, West Virginia 26651
(304) 872-0825 / www.carnifexferrybattlefieldstatepark.com/
Union forces retained control of the Kanawha Valley after this 1861 victory.

Droop Mountain Battlefield State Park
HC 64 Box 189, Hillsboro, West Virginia 24946
www.droopmountainbattlefield.com/
The Union victory ended Confederate operations in West Virginia.

Harpers Ferry National Historical Park
171 Shoreline Dr., Harpers Ferry, West Virginia 25425
(304) 535-6029 / www.nps.gov/hafe/index.htm
Site of John Brown's 1859 raid and 1862 battle during the Maryland Campaign.

Wisconsin

Civil War Museum of the Upper Middle West
5400 1st Avenue, Kenosha, Wisconsin 53140. www.kenosha.org/civilwar/
Explores the home front in Wis., Ind., Mich., Ill., Ia., and Minn. during the Civil War.

Index

African Americans, 6

African-American prisoners, 71

Alabama Military Units: 4th Cavalry, 102; 6th Infantry, 102; 19th Infantry, 101

Alexander, W. A., 60

Altman, Sampson Jr., 105

amputation, 67

Anderson, Gen. George, 48

Anderson, Maj. Robert, 2

Andersonville prison, 22, 75

Anthony, Sgt. John W., 128

antibiotics, 66

Antietam, battle of, 20-21, 41-43, 70, 111

Appomattox Court House, 24, 38, 94-96, 118, 122, 128, 130

Arkansas Military Units: 2nd Infantry, 103; 3rd Infantry, 4; 4th Infantry, 103; 8th Regiment, Militia, 4; 24th Infantry, 103

Arlington Confederate Monument, 100

Arlington National Cemetery, 100, 134

Armstrong cannon, 36

Army of Central Kentucky, 18

Army of Louisiana, 18

Army of Mississippi, 18

Army of Missouri, 18

Army of New Mexico, 18

Army of Northern Virginia, 18, 24, 39, 44, 51, 92, 94, 119, 122

Army of Pensacola, 18, 51

Army of Tennessee, 18-19, 50, 54

Army of the Cumberland, 50

Army of the Mississippi, 18

Army of the Ohio, 54

Army of the Potomac, 44, 46, 92

Army of the South, 19

Army of the Tennessee, 24, 49, 52

Army of the Valley, 19

Army of the West, 18

Atlanta, battle of, 23, 53-54, 57, 90

Augusta (Georgia) Powder Works, 58

Averasboro, battle of, 24

bacteria, 67

Baker's Creek, battle of, 22, 108, 115

Ball's Bluff, battle of, 21

Banks, Gen. Nathaniel, 67

Barksdale, Gen. William, 111

Bates, Pvt. Thomas F., 125

Baton Rouge, Louisiana, 91

Battery Wagner, battle of, 22

"The Battle Above the Clouds," 50

Beauregard, Gen. P. G. T., 2-3, 18, 38

Belle Grove, battle of, 23

Belle Isle prison, 72

Benson, Sgt. Berry, 120

Bentonville, battle of, 19, 24, 93, 104, 108

Biedler, William T., 134

Big Bethel, battle of, 20, 111, 116

Blake, Pvt. William Billy, 111

Bolding, Thomas, 103

"Bounty Jumpers," 25

Bowen, Thomas, 124

Box, Sgt. James R., 126

Boyd, Belle, 88

Bragg, Gen. Braxton, 18-19, 21, 50

Branch, Gen. Lawrence O., 117

Breckinridge, Gen. John C., 91

Brice's Cross Roads, battle of, 23

Bristoe Station, battle of, 112

Buchanan, Franklin, 83

Bull Run, First battle of, 5, 20, 38, 41, 110, 128

Bull Run, Second battle of, 21

Burnside, Gen. Ambrose, 43-44

Camp Chase prison, 105

Camp Douglas prison, 75, 107, 114

camp life, 11

Camp Morton prison, 102, 107, 123

Cane Hill, battle of, 135

Carey, Pvt. Edward A., 129

Carpetbaggers, 98

Carter, John L., 102

Casey, Pvt. Parris P., 101

Castle Pinckney, 11

casualties (chart), 26

Cedar Creek, battle of, 23, 118

Cedar Mountain, Virginia, 67

Centreville, Virginia, 12

Champion Hill, battle of, 22, 108, 115

Chancellorsville, battle of, 21, 39, 45, 105-106, 118-119

Charleston, South Carolina, 2-3, 8, 20, 22, 63, 67, 78, 121, 124

Chattanooga, siege of, 22, 41, 50

Chattanooga, Tennessee, 69

Chickamauga, battle of, 22, 41, 50, 102

Chimborazo hospital, 68, 131

Civil War, cause of, 1

Clapp, Pvt. Luther H., 134

Colbert, David C., 128

Cold Harbor, battle of, 22, 39, 130

Columbia, South Carolina, 20, 24

Columbus, Kentucky, 114

Commissary Department, 19

Compiled Service Records of Confederate General and Staff Officers, 138

Confederate Military Units: 1st Cavalry, 7

consumption, 66

Cook, Henry Howe, 124

Cook, Philip, 105

Corinth, battle of, 18, 21

Corinth, Mississippi, 29, 45, 69, 115

Crater, battle of the, 23, 35

Crow's Factory Hospital, 131

Crump, Pleasant, 136
CSS *Alabama*, 23, 78
CSS *Atlanta*, 59
CSS *Chicora*, 59, 81
CSS *Fredericksburg*, 94
CSS *General* Bragg, 81
CSS *Palmetto State*, 59
CSS *Richmond*, 94
CSS *Robert E. Lee*, 82
CSS *Shenandoah*, 24, 78, 84, 94
CSS *Teaser*, 80
CSS *Tennessee*, 83
CSS *Virginia*, 21, 78, 83
CSS *Virginia II*, 94
Culp's Hill, 46
Cumming, Kate, 69
Cunningham, Sgt. Sumner A., 123
Davis, Jefferson, 20, 24, 58, 78
Devil's Den, 47
diarrhea, 66
Dinkins, James, 111
Dix, Gen. John A., 71
Dix-Hill Cartel, 71-73
Dodd, Pvt. James, 119
Draft Riots, 22
Drewry's Bluff, Virginia, 65, 124
Duvall, David H., 114-115
Duvall, Thomas, 115
Duvall, William, 115
dysentery, 66
Early, Gen. Jubal A., 19, 130
electric torpedo, 83
Elkhorn Tavern, battle of, 21, 41, 103, 113, 115
Elmira prison, 75, 116, 120
Emancipation Proclamation, 21, 89
Enfield Rifled Musket, 32-34
Estopinal, Albert, 108
Ezekiel, Moses, 134
Ezra Church, battle of, 53
Fair Oaks, battle of, 21, 40, 66
Fayetteville Rifled Musket, 34
Fayetteville, North Carolina, 24
Fisher's Hill, battle of, 23, 130
Five Forks, battle of, 24, 73, 93, 128
Flynt, James McDavid, 103
food riots, 86
Forrest, Gen. Nathan B., 97, 102, 111,
Fort Columbus prison, 118
Fort Darling, 65
Fort Delaware prison, 106, 123, 130

Fort Donelson, battle of, 21, 39, 123
Fort Fisher, battle of, 23, 36, 54, 62
Fort Harrison, battle of, 23
Fort Henry, battle of, 21, 39
Fort Johnson, South Carolina, 63
Fort Mahone, Virginia, 93
Fort McAllister, Georgia, 56
Fort Pillow, battle of, 22
Fort Pulaski, Georgia, 61-62
Fort Stedman, Virginia, 24, 105
Fort Sumter, South Carolina, 1-3, 11, 20, 24, 62-64
Fort Tyler, Alabama, 62
Franklin, battle of, 23, 54, 104, 123
Franklin, Pvt. Eli, 119
Fredericksburg, Virginia, 21, 39, 44, 92, 111, 118
gabions, 64
Gaines' Mill, battle of, 40
Garland, Emma Carey, 129
Georgia Military Units: 4th Infantry, 105-106; 8th Cavalry, 120; 29th Infantry, 105; 40th Infantry, 104-105; 41st Infantry, 104; Hampton Legion, 120
Gettys, Alphonso E., 122
Gettysburg, battle of, 6, 13, 22, 41, 46-48, 73, 77, 99-100, 102, 105-106, 110-111, 116, 130
Gibbs, George E., 114
Goodson, Reuben, 113
Gosport Naval Yard, 78
Grant, Gen. Ulysses S., 22, 38-39, 44, 49, 51-52, 93-95
Graves, Bernard B., 130
Graves, Sallie Hunt, 131
Green, Ellis, 121
Hampton Roads, battle of, 21
hand grenades, 35
Hanover Court House, battle of, 118
Harbison, Pvt. W. T., 116
Harpers Ferry, Virginia, 33-34, 42
Harris, Col. Nathaniel, 112
Hart, Nancy, 88
Hatcher's Run, battle of, 110
Hill, David J., 110
Hill, Gen. A. P., 43
Hill, Gen. D. H., 71
Holly Springs, Mississippi, 49
Hollywood Cemetery, 48
Hood, Gen. John Bell, 54, 66

Hooker, Gen. Joseph "Fighting Joe," 45
Hoover, Betty, 30
Hughes, Andrew J., 118
H. L. Hunley, 22, 60, 78
Hurd, Dr. Anson, 70
Immortal Six Hundred, 124
Indian Home Guard, 135
Indiana Military Units: 14th Infantry, 70
infection, 67
inflation, 86
ironclad ships, 59, 78
Island No. 10, 114
Iuka, battle of, 115
Jackson, Gen. Thomas J. "Stonewall," 14, 21, 42, 45, 67, 118, 133
Jackson, Mississippi, 108
James, Frank and Jesse, 89
James, Zerelda, 89
Jefferson Barracks, Missouri, 72
Jefferson, Thomas Garland, 133
Johnson, R. Cecile, 120
Johnson's Island prison, 72
Johnston, Gen. Albert S., 18, 44
Johnston, Gen. Joseph E., 18-19, 40, 52-53, 93-94, 96
Jones, Catesby, 83
Kennesaw Mountain, battle of, 23, 52-53
Kentucky Military Unit, 3rd Cavalry, 107
Kernstown, battle of, 133
King, John H., 105
Knoxville, siege of, 22
Kurtz, Pvt. Peter Lauck, 130
Lacy, Beverly Tucker, 13
Ladies Memorial Association, 98-99
land mines, 35, 60
Landvoigt, Pvt. Ed, 7
LaRoque, John G., 106
LaRoque, Nancy, 106
Las Moras, Texas, 15
Lee, Gen. Robert E., 13, 19, 21, 24, 38-39, 42, 45-46, 51-52, 92-96, 106, 112, 117, 119, 122
Lee, John, 125
Leon, Louis, 116
Lexington, Missouri, 21
Libby prison, 72

Licks, Lewis, 117
Lincoln, Abraham, 1; calls up 75,000 volunteers, 2; refuses the legality of secession, 2; calls up 500,000 men, 5; elected president, 20; Gettysburg Address, 22; reelected, 23; assassinated, 24
Little Round Top, 47
Logan's Cross Roads, battle of, 21
Lookout Mountain, battle of, 22, 50
Lost Cause, 98
Louisiana Military Units: 3rd Infantry, 13; 7th Battalion Infantry, 110; 12th Infantry, 108; 22nd Infantry, 108; 28th Infantry, 108; Washington Artillery, 3rd Company, 109; Zouave Battalion, 110
Louisville military prison, 107
Love, Pvt. Lucien, 135
Lowry, Pvt. David, 133
Lumpkin, Cincinnatus, 131
Lumpkin, Henry T., 131
Lumpkin, Tomley, 131
Lumpkin, Theodore F., 131
Mallory, Stephen M., 59, 78-79
Malvern Hill, battle of, 128
Manassas, First battle of, 11, 20, 38, 110, 128
Manassas, Second battle of, 21, 39, 41-42, 111
Mann, Theophilus, 130
Mansfield, battle of, 22, 126
"March to the Sea," 23, 86
Martin, Albert B., 109
Maury, Matthew Fontaine, 83
Mayo, Charles, 102
Mayo, William, 102
McCaw, James B., 68
McClellan, Gen. George B., 40
McCreary, Thomas, 107
McLean, Wilmer, 38, 95
Meade, Gen. George G., 46, 51
measles, 66
medical care, 66
Memphis, Tennessee, 21
Mill Springs, battle of, 21
Millner, Sgt. James W., 128
Minié Ball, 32-33
Minié, Claude-Etienne, 33
Missionary Ridge, battle of, 22, 50

Mississippi Military Units: 2nd Infantry, 110; 15th Infantry, 112; 16th Infantry, 112; 18th Infantry, 111; 19th Infantry, 112; 43rd Infantry, 14
Missouri Military Units: 1st Cavalry, 113; 3rd Infantry, 115; 5th Infantry, 113; State Guard, 114-115
Mobile Bay, battle of, 23, 83
Monocacy, battle of, 23
Moore, Col. W. H., 14
Moore, Henry A., 112
Morgan, Gen. John Hunt, 102, 107
Mosby, Charles B., 132
Mosby, Maj. John S., 134
Mosby's Rangers, 134-135
Murfreesboro, battle of, 21, 41, 103, 124
Napoleon 12-lb cannon, 37
Nashville, battle of, 23, 54, 104
Nashville, Tennessee, 69
Natchez, Mississippi, 3
National Archives, 137-138
Naval Affairs Committee, 78
New Market, battle of, 22, 133-134
New Mexico, Pecos National Historical Park, Pecos, 152
New Mexico Campaign, 18
New Orleans, Louisiana, 8, 21
Nicholson, James W., 108
North Carolina Military Units: 1st Infantry, 111, 116; 3rd Infantry, 117; 4th Infantry, 118; 11th Infantry, 116; 12th Infantry, 118; 13th Infantry, 117; 18th Infantry, 117; 52nd Infantry, 113; 53rd Infantry, 116-117
Oak Hills, battle of, 4, 20, 39, 41, 89, 110, 115
Old Capitol Prison, 71, 120, 131
Olmstead, Charles H., 61
"On to Richmond," 38
Ordnance Department, 19
Paine, Halbert E., 91
Palmito Ranch, engagement at, 24
Pea Ridge, battle of, 21, 41, 103, 113, 115
Peachtree Creek, battle of, 23, 53
Pemberton, John C., 49
Perryville, battle of, 18, 21, 41, 103-104

Petersburg, Virginia, 23, 53, 93-95
photography, 27-28
Pickett's Charge, 6, 99
Pittsburg Landing, battle of, 21
Pleasant Hill, battle of, 22, 126
pneumonia, 66
Pohle, Drum Major Carl R. M., 132
Point Lookout prison, 72, 80, 116, 123
Pope, Gen. John, 114
Point Lookout, Maryland, 131
Port Hudson, Louisiana, 12, 22, 41, 65
Port Republic, battle of, 129
Porter, Felicia, 69
Posey, Gen. Carnot, 112
Prairie Grove, battle of, 135
Price, Gen. Sterling, 18, 115
"Quaker gun," 37
Quantrill, William C., 89
Quartermaster Department, 19
railroads, 55, 57
Rains, George Washington, 58
Rapier, John L., 110
Ray, Rhoda, 89
Ream's Station, battle of, 23
Red River Campaign, 22, 126
religion, 13
Renwick, John P., 110
Resaca, battle of, 22
Richmond National Battlefield, 55
Richmond, Virginia, 65, 94-95
Ritchie, Col. John, 135
Roanoke Island, North Carolina, 21
Rock Island prison, 76
Rockwell, Pvt. William H., 117
Roper Hospital, 67
Rosecrans, Gen. William S., 50
Sabine Crossroads, battle of, 22
Sabine Pass, battle of, 126
Sailor's Creek, battle of, 24
Samuel, Dr. Reuben, 89
sanitation, 66

Savage, John C., 127
Savage, William, 127
Savannah, Georgia, 56, 59, 61-62
Sayler's Creek, Battle of, 94-95
Scofield, Gen. John, 54
Secession Convention, 20
"see the elephant," 6, 10
Senate Committee on Naval Affairs, 79
Seven Days' battles, 21, 39, 111, 117-118, 128
Seven Pines, battle of, 18, 21, 40, 66, 128, 131
Sevierville, Tennessee, engagement at, 105
sharecropping, 98
Sharpsburg, battle of, 20, 21, 41-43, 70, 111
Shenandoah Valley Campaign, 74
Sherman, Gen. William T., 23, 41, 52, 56, 86, 96
Shiloh, battle of, 18, 21, 41, 44, 69
Shirley, Pvt. Silas A., 112
"Sibley Brigade," 18
Sibley, Gen. Henry, 18
signal system, 56
Simmons, Pvt. John, 126
slavery, 1
smallpox, 66
Smith, Gen. Edmund K., 96
South Carolina Military Units: 1st Infantry, 119-120; 4th Cavalry, 119; 5th Infantry, 122; 30th Infantry, 121; McCellan Zouaves, 121
Southern Confederacy, population, 1
Southern men, 2, 8
Southside Railroad, 93
Spanish Fort, battle of, 126
Spotsylvania Court House, battle of, 22, 39, 70, 106, 112, 118, 120
Spring Hill, battle of, 54
Springfield 1861 Rifled Musket, 34
SS Fingal, 59
SS Ruby, 82
Steele, Gen. Frederick, 126
Stikeleather, John, 118
Stone's River, battle of, 21, 124
Stonewall Brigade, 16
Stuart, Gen. James E. B., 22
Sumter Military Prison, 75
Sweet, Jonathan, 14
Taylor, Gen. Richard, 24, 96

Templeton, Sarah, 122
Tennessee Military Units: 1st Infantry, 124; 41st Infantry, 123; 44th Infantry, 124; 60th Mounted Infantry, 123; Zollicoffer Mounted Rifles, 124
Texas Brigade, 16
Texas Military Units: 6th Infantry, 125; 14th Cavalry, 126; 22nd Infantry, 125
Thomas, Gen. George H., 54
Timrod, Henry, 121
Timrod, Henry, 125
Toombs, Gen. Robert, 43
torpedoes, 35
Trans-Mississippi Theater, 41
Tredegar Iron Works, 55
Tupelo, Mississippi, 23
typhoid fever, 66
Upperville, battle of, 120
USS Cairo, 78
USS Fort Donelson, 82
USS Houstonic, 22, 60
USS Kearsarge, 23
USS Maratanza, 80
USS Merrimack, 78
USS Monitor, 21, 78, 83
USS Weehawken, 59
Veteran Reserve Corps, 25
Vicksburg, siege of, 13, 14, 22, 35, 41, 49, 65, 104-105, 108, 123, 126
Virginia Military Institute, 22, 133
Virginia Military Units: 1st Infantry, 132; 5th Infantry, 130; 6th Cavalry, 131; 11th Infantry, 128; 15th Infantry, 127; 25th Mounted Rifles, 133; 34th Infantry, 131; 37th Infantry, 133-134; 38th Infantry, 128; 41st Militia, 133; 43rd Battalion, 134; 44th Infantry, 129; 46th Infantry, 128; 59th Infantry, 13; Farinholt's Infantry Battalion, 130; Henderson's Heavy Artillery, 132; Light Artillery (Amherst Artillery), 130; Light Artillery (Hanover Artillery), 130; Light Artillery Battery, 127; Richmond Howitzers, 14
Walker, Gen. John, 126
Ward, William P., 104

Washington (Louisiana) Light Artillery, 10
Watie, Gen. Stand, 24, 94
Waynesboro, battle of, 19
Weldon Railroad, 23
Whetstone, Jacob, 103
White, James Bishop, 123
Whitehead, John R., 131
Wilderness, battle of, 22, 39, 51-52, 112, 116, 118
Williams, Walter, 136
Wilmington, North Carolina, 24, 54, 62, 82
Wilson, Woodrow, 100
Wilson's Creek, battle of, 4, 20, 39, 41, 89, 110, 115
Winchester, Third battle of, 23, 117
Women enlisting in the army, 6
women in the war, 85, 86
Women's Relief Society, 69
Wright, Joseph D., 113
Wyeth, John, 102
Yellow Tavern, battle of, 22
Yorktown, battle of, 40
Zigler, Mollie Knopp, 30

About the Author

Mark Hughes is widely recognized as the authority on Civil War cemeteries. The only author to publish books on both Union and Confederate cemeteries, his titles include: *Bivouac of the Dead, The Unpublished Roll of Honor*, and *Confederate Cemeteries* (2 vols.). His bestselling *The New Civil War Handbook* (2009) has been hailed as "a long overdue update of a classic." Mark has also written articles on a variety of subjects.

Mark is a retired electronics technologist who worked in the electronics field for 43 years. For 28 years he was a college department head and an instructor of Electronic Engineering Technology. He is a graduate of Gaston College (AAS) and Southeastern Oklahoma State University (BS and Masters of Technology). In 2017, Southeastern Oklahoma State University honored Hughes as a Distinguished Alumni.

Mark, his wife Patty, and their daughter Anna Grace live on the family farm near Kings Mountain, North Carolina.